日本語能力試験
AF505782
JAPANESE-LANGUAGE
PROFICIENCY TEST
Full N1-N5 Kanji Vocabulary List
Japanese - English - Chinese
Nihongo Tutors has been the most trusted tutoring
institution in the area for over 3 years. We won't fail you!

日 N5	**一** N5	**国** N5	**人** N5
day, sun, Japan	one	country	person
天	一	国家	人
年 N5	**大** N5	**十** N5	**二** N5
year	large, big	ten	two
年	大	十	二
本 N5	**中** N5	**長** N5	**出** N5
book, present, main, true, real	in, inside, middle, mean, center	long, leader	exit, leave
这个	在	长	出
三 N5	**時** N5	**行** N5	**見** N5
three	time, hour	going, journey	see, hopes, chances, idea, opinion, look at, visible
三	时间	行	看到
月 N5	**後** N5	**前** N5	**五** N5
month, moon	behind, back, later	in front, before	five
月	后	之前	五人制

N5	N5	N5	N5
間	**上**	**東**	**四**
interval, space	above, up	east	four
之间	上	东	四
今	**金**	**九**	**入**
now	gold	nine	enter, insert
现在	金	九	输入
学	**高**	**円**	**子**
study, learning, science	tall, high, expensive	circle, yen, round	child, sign of the rat, 11PM-1AM
研究	高	圈	儿童
外	**八**	**六**	**下**
outside	eight	six	below, down, descend, give, low, inferior
外	八	六	下面
来	**気**	**小**	**七**
come, due, next, cause, become	spirit, mind	little, small	seven
来	精神	小	七

山 N5	話 N5	女 N5	北 N5
mountain	tale, talk	woman, female	north
山	故事	女人	北
午 N5	百 N5	書 N5	先 N5
noon, sign of the horse, 11AM-1PM	hundred	write	before, ahead, previous, future, precedence
中午	百	写	之前
名 N5	川 N5	千 N5	水 N5
name, noted, distinguished, reputation	stream, river	thousand	water
名称	河	千	水
半 N5	男 N5	西 N5	電 N5
half, middle, odd number, semi-, part-half	male	west, Spain	electricity
半	男	西方	电力
校 N5	語 N5	土 N5	木 N5
exam, school, printing, proof, correction	word, speech, language	soil, earth, ground, Turkey	tree, wood
考试	言语	泥	树

聞 N5	食 N5	車 N5	何 N5
hear, ask, listen	eat, food	car	what
听	吃	汽车	什么
南 N5	万 N5	毎 N5	白 N5
south	ten thousand	every	white
南	万	每一个	白色
天 N5	母 N5	火 N5	右 N5
heavens, sky, imperial	mama, mother	fire	right
天空	母亲	火	对
読 N5	友 N5	左 N5	休 N5
read	friend	left	rest, day off, retire, sleep
读	朋友	剩下	退休
父 N5	雨 N5	会 N5	同 N5
father	rain	meeting, meet, party, association, interview, join	same, agree, equal
父亲	雨	派对	同意

事 N4 matter, thing, fact, business, reason, possibly 事实	**自** N4 oneself 自己	**社** N4 company, firm, office, association, shrine 公司	**発** N4 discharge, departure, publish, emit, start from 排出
者 N4 someone, person 人	**地** N4 ground, earth 地球	**業** N4 business, vocation, arts, performance 商业	**方** N4 direction, person, alternative 方向
新 N4 new 新	**場** N4 location, place 位置	**員** N4 employee, member, number, the one in charge 雇员	**立** N4 stand up 站起来
開 N4 open, unfold, unseal 打开	**手** N4 hand 手	**力** N4 power, strong, strain, bear up, exert 力	**問** N4 question, ask, problem 问
代 N4 substitute, change, convert, replace, period 代	**明** N4 bright, light 亮	**動** N4 move, motion, change, confusion, shift, shake 移动	**京** N4 capital 北京

N4	N4	N4	N4
目	通	言	理
eye, class, look, insight, experience, care, favor	traffic, pass through, avenue, commute	say	logic, arrangement, reason, justice, truth
头	通过	言语	原因
体	田	主	題
body, substance, object, reality, counter for images	rice field, rice paddy	lord, chief, master, main thing, principal	topic, subject
身体	领域	主	题
意	不	作	用
idea, mind, heart, taste, thought, desire	negative, non-, bad, ugly, clumsy	make, production, prepare, build	utilize, business, service, use, employ
含义	不要	使	采用
度	強	公	持
degrees, occurrence, time, counter for occurrences	strong	public, prince, official, governmental	hold, have
学位	强大	上市	保持
野	以	思	家
plains, field, rustic, civilian life	by means of, because, in view of, compared with	think	house, home
野生	至	认为	家庭

世 N4	多 N4	正 N4	院 N4
generation, world, society, public	many, frequent, much	correct, justice, righteous, 10**40	Inst., institution, temple, mansion, school
世界	许多	正	医院
心 N4	界 N4	教 N4	文 N4
heart, mind, spirit	world	teach, faith, doctrine	sentence, literature, style, art, decoration
心	边界	教	文本
元 N4	重 N4	近 N4	考 N4
beginning, former time, origin	heavy, heap up, pile up, nest of boxes, -fold	near, early, akin, tantamount	consider, think over
元	重量	近	测试
画 N4	海 N4	売 N4	知 N4
brush-stroke, picture	sea, ocean	sell	know, wisdom
绘画	海	卖	知道
道 N4	集 N4	别 N4	物 N4
road-way, street, district, journey, course	gather, meet, congregate, swarm, flock	separate, branch off, diverge, fork, another	thing, object, matter
路	收集	分离	宾语

使 N4	品 N4	計 N4	死 N4
use	goods, refinement, dignity, article	plot, plan, scheme, measure	death, die
采用	产品	方案	死
特 N4	私 N4	始 N4	朝 N4
special	private, I, me	commence, begin	morning, dynasty, regime, epoch, period
特别	私人的	开始	向
運 N4	終 N4	台 N4	広 N4
carry, luck, destiny, fate, lot, transport	end, finish	pedestal, a stand, counter for machines and vehicles	wide, broad, spacious
运输	结束	站	宽
住 N4	真 N4	有 N4	口 N4
dwell, reside, live, inhabit	true, reality, Buddhist sect	possess, have, exist, happen, occur, approx	mouth
住	现实	具有	口
少 N4	町 N4	料 N4	工 N4
few, little	village, town, block, street	fee, materials	craft, construction
减	村	材料	工艺

建 N4 build 建立	**空** N4 empty, sky, void, vacant, vacuum 天空	**急** N4 hurry, emergency, sudden, steep 匆忙	**止** N4 stop, halt 停
送 N4 escort, send 护送	**切** N4 cut, cutoff, be sharp 隔断	**転** N4 revolve, turn around, change 围绕	**研** N4 polish, study of, sharpen 研究
足 N4 leg, foot, be sufficient 脚丫子	**究** N4 research, study 研究	**楽** N4 music, comfort, ease 音乐	**起** N4 rouse, wake up, get up 醒来
着 N4 arrive, wear, counter for suits of clothing 到达	**店** N4 store, shop 商店	**病** N4 ill, sick 生病	**質** N4 substance, quality, matter, temperament 质量
待 N4 wait, depend on 等待	**試** N4 test, try, attempt, experiment, ordeal 测试	**族** N4 tribe, family 家庭	**銀** N4 silver 银

早 N4 early, fast 早	**映** N4 reflect, reflection, projection 反映	**親** N4 parent, intimacy, relative, familiarity 父母	**験** N4 verification, effect, testing 影响
英 N4 England, English 英语	**医** N4 doctor, medicine 医疗	**仕** N4 attend, doing, official, serve 官方	**去** N4 gone, past, quit, leave, elapse, eliminate, divorce 放弃
味 N4 flavor, taste 味道	**写** N4 copy, be photographed, describe 复制	**字** N4 character, letter, word, section of village 字符	**答** N4 solution, answer 回答
夜 N4 night, evening 晚	**音** N4 sound, noise 声音	**注** N4 pour, irrigate, shed (tears), flow into 灌溉	**帰** N4 homecoming, arrive at, lead to, result in 归乡
古 N4 old 古	**歌** N4 song, sing 歌曲	**買** N4 buy 购买	**悪** N4 bad, vice, rascal, false, evil, wrong 坏

N4	N4	N4	N4
図 map, drawing, plan, unexpected, accidentally 地图	**週** week 周	**室** room, apartment, chamber, greenhouse, cellar 房间	**歩** walk, counter for steps 步行
風 wind, air, style, manner 风	**紙** paper 纸	**黒** black 黑色	**花** flower 花
春 springtime, spring (season) 弹簧	**赤** red 红色	**青** blue, green 绿色	**館** building, mansion, large building, palace 建造
屋 roof, house, shop, dealer, seller 屋	**色** color 颜色	**走** run 跑	**秋** autumn 秋季
夏 summer 夏天	**習** learn 研究	**駅** station 站	**洋** ocean, western style 海洋

旅 N4 trip, travel 旅行	**服** N4 clothing, admit, obey, discharge 衣服	**夕** N4 evening 晚间	**借** N4 borrow, rent 借
曜 N4 weekday 平日	**飲** N4 drink, smoke, take 喝	**肉** N4 meat 肉	**貸** N4 lend 借
堂 N4 public chamber, hall 大厅	**鳥** N4 bird, chicken 鸟	**飯** N4 meal, boiled rice 白饭	**勉** N4 exertion 用力
冬 N4 winter 冬季	**昼** N4 daytime, noon 白天	**茶** N4 tea 茶	**牛** N4 cow 牛
魚 N4 fish 鱼	**兄** N4 elder brother, big brother 哥哥	**犬** N4 dog 狗	**漢** N4 Sino-, China 中文

政 N3	議 N3	民 N3	連 N3
politics, government	deliberation, consultation, debate, consideration	people, nation, subjects	take along, lead, join, connect, party, gang, clique
政府	讨论	人	加入
対 N3	部 N3	合 N3	市 N3
vis-a-vis, opposite, even, equal, versus, anti-	section, bureau, dept, class, copy, part	fit, suit, join	market, city, town
相反	部分	适合	市
内 N3	相 N3	定 N3	回 N3
inside, within, between, among, house, home	inter-, mutual, together, each other	determine, fix, establish, decide	-times, round, game, revolve
内	一起	建立	围绕
選 N3	米 N3	実 N3	関 N3
elect, select, choose, prefer	rice, USA, metre	reality, truth	connection, barrier, gateway, involve, concerning
选	仪表	真相	屏障
決 N3	全 N3	表 N3	戦 N3
decide, fix, agree upon, appoint	whole, entire, all, complete, fulfill	surface, table, chart, diagram	war, battle, match
决定	所有	表	战斗

N3	N3	N3	N3
経	**最**	**現**	**調**
sutra, longitude, pass thru, expire, warp	utmost, most, extreme	present, existing, actual	tune, tone, meter, key (music), writing style
到期	最	当下	调
化	**当**	**約**	**首**
change, take the form of, influence, enchant	hit, right, appropriate, himself	promise, approximately, shrink	neck
更改	击中	大约	颈部
法	**性**	**要**	**制**
method, law, rule, principle, model, system	sex, gender, nature	need, main point, essence, pivot, key to	system, law, rule
法	性别	需要	系统
治	**務**	**成**	**期**
reign, be at peace, calm down, subdue, quell	task, duties	turn into, become, get, grow, elapse, reach	period, time, date, term
统治	任务	成为	期
取	**都**	**和**	**機**
take, fetch, take up	metropolis, capital	harmony, Japanese style, peace, soften, Japan	mechanism, opportunity, occasion, machine, airplane
取	首都	和谐	机

平 N3	加 N3	受 N3	続 N3
even, flat, peace	add, addition, increase, join, include, Canada	accept, undergo, answer (phone), take, get	continue, series, sequel
水平	加成	接受	继续
進 N3	数 N3	記 N3	初 N3
advance, proceed, progress, promote	number, strength, fate, law, figures	scribe, account, narrative	first time, beginning
预先	数	隶	早
指 N3	権 N3	支 N3	産 N3
finger, point to, indicate, put into, play (chess)	authority, power, rights	branch, support, sustain	products, bear, give birth, yield, childbirth
表明	权威	支持	生产
点 N3	報 N3	済 N3	活 N3
spot, point, mark, speck, decimal point	report, news, reward, retribution	finish, come to an end, excusable, need not	lively, resuscitation, being helped, living
点	报告	完	活泼
原 N3	共 N3	得 N3	解 N3
meadow, original, primitive, field, plain	together, both, neither, all, and, alike, with	gain, get, find, earn, acquire, can, may	unravel, notes, key, explanation
原版的	一起	获得	解

交 N3 mingle, mixing, association, coming & going 协会	**資** N3 assets, resources, capital, funds, data 资源	**予** N3 beforehand, previous, myself, I 预先	**向** N3 yonder, facing, beyond, confront, defy 超越
際 N3 occasion, side, edge, verge, dangerous, adventurous 场合	**勝** N3 victory, win, prevail, excel 赢得	**面** N3 mask, face, features, surface 表面	**告** N3 revelation, tell, inform, announce 宣布
反 N3 anti- 抗	**判** N3 judgement, signature, stamp, seal 判断	**認** N3 acknowledge, witness, discern, recognize 认识	**参** N3 nonplussed, three, going, coming, visiting 参加
利 N3 profit, advantage, benefit 利润	**組** N3 association, braid, plait, construct, assemble 协会	**信** N3 faith, truth, fidelity, trust 信仰	**在** N3 exist, outskirts, suburbs, located in 存在
件 N3 affair, case, matter, item 事务	**側** N3 side, lean, oppose, regret 侧	**任** N3 responsibility, duty, term, entrust to, appoint 责任	**引** N3 pull, tug, jerk, admit, install, quote, refer to 拉

N3	N3	N3	N3
求	**所**	**次**	**昨**
request, want, wish for, require, demand	place	next, order, sequence	yesterday, previous
請求	地点	顺序	昨天
論	**官**	**増**	**係**
argument, discourse	bureaucrat, the government	increase, add, augment, gain, promote	person in charge, connection, duty, concern oneself
论点	官僚	增加	义务
感	**情**	**投**	**示**
emotion, feeling, sensation	feelings, emotion, passion, sympathy	throw, discard, abandon, launch into, join	show, indicate, point out, express, display
情感	情怀	丢弃	表明
変	**打**	**直**	**両**
unusual, change, strange	strike, hit, knock, pound, dozen	straightaway, honesty, frankness, fix, repair	both, old Japanese coin, counter for vehicles, two
奇怪	罢工	诚实	都
式	**確**	**果**	**容**
style, ceremony, rite, function, method, system	assurance, firm, tight, hard, solid, confirm	fruit, reward, carry out, achieve, complete, end	contain, form, looks
仪式	保证	水果	包含

必

invariably, certain, inevitable

必然

演

performance, act, play, render, stage

性能

歳

year-end, age, occasion, opportunity

场合

争

contend, dispute, argue

争议

談

discuss, talk

谈论

能

ability, talent, skill, capacity

技能

位

rank, grade, throne, crown, about, some

秩

置

placement, put, set, deposit, leave behind

放置

流

current, a sink, flow, forfeit

当前

格

status, rank, capacity, character

状态

疑

doubt, distrust, be suspicious, question

疑似

過

overdo, exceed, go beyond, error

超过

局

bureau, board, office, affair, conclusion

局

放

set free, release, fire, shoot, emit, banish

发布

常

usual, ordinary, normal, regular

普通

状

status quo, conditions, circumstances, form

情况

球

ball, sphere

球

職

post, employment, work

工作

与

bestow, participate in, give, award, impart, provide

与

供

submit, offer, present, serve (meal), accompany

提交

N3	N3	N3	N3
役	**構**	**割**	**費**
duty, war, campaign, drafted labor, office, service	posture, build, pretend	proportion, comparatively, divide, cut, separate	expense, cost, spend, consume, waste
义务	姿势	比例	费用
付	**由**	**説**	**難**
adhere, attach, refer to, append	wherefore, a reason	rumor, opinion, theory	difficult, impossible, trouble, accident, defect
坚持	原因	谣言	难
優	**夫**	**収**	**断**
tenderness, excel, surpass, actor, superiority	husband, man	income, obtain, reap, pay, supply, store	severance, decline, refuse, apologize
优秀	丈夫	收入	遣散费
石	**違**	**消**	**神**
stone	difference, differ	extinguish, blow out, turn off, neutralize, cancel	gods, mind, soul
石	区别	扑灭	神
番	**規**	**術**	**備**
turn, number in a series	standard, measure	art, technique, skill, means, trick, resources	equip, provision, preparation
转	标准	技术	准备

宅 N3 home, house, residence, our house, my husband 屋	**害** N3 harm, injury 危害	**配** N3 distribute, spouse, exile, rationing 分发	**警** N3 admonish, commandment 谏
育 N3 bring up, grow up, raise, rear 提高	**席** N3 seat, mat, occasion, place 座位	**訪** N3 call on, visit, look up, offer sympathy 访问	**乗** N3 ride, power, multiplication, record 乘
残 N3 remainder, leftover, balance 剩下的	**想** N3 concept, think, idea, thought 概念	**声** N3 voice 声音	**念** N3 wish, sense, idea, thought, feeling, desire 希望
助 N3 help, rescue, assist 救命	**労** N3 labor, thank for, reward for, toil, trouble 劳工	**例** N3 example, custom, usage, precedent 例	**然** N3 sort of thing, so, if so, in that case, well 当然
限 N3 limit, restrict, to best of ability 限制	**追** N3 chase, drive away, follow, pursue, meanwhile 追	**商** N3 make a deal, selling, dealing in, merchant 商人	**葉** N3 leaf, plane, lobe, needle, blade, spear 叶

N3	N3	N3	N3
伝	**働**	**形**	**景**
transmit, go along, walk along, follow, report	work, (kokuji)	shape, form, style	scenery, view
发送	工作	形成	风景
好	**退**	**頭**	**負**
fond, pleasing, like something	retreat, withdraw, retire, resign, repel, expel	head, counter for large animals	defeat, negative, -, minus, bear, owe
赏心悦目	撤退	头	负
渡	**失**	**差**	**末**
transit, ford, ferry, cross, import, deliver	lose, error, fault, disadvantage, loss	distinction, difference, variation, discrepancy	end, close, tip, powder, posterity
过境	失利	区别	结束
守	**若**	**種**	**美**
guard, protect, defend, obey	young, if, perhaps, possibly, low number, immature	species, kind, class, variety, seed	beauty, beautiful
防御	年轻	种子	美人
命	**福**	**望**	**非**
fate, command, decree, destiny, life, appoint	blessing, fortune, luck, wealth	ambition, full moon, hope, desire, aspire to, expect	un-, mistake, negative, injustice, non-
生活	祝福	野心	错误

観 (N3) outlook, look, appearance, condition, view 出现	**察** (N3) guess, presume, surmise, judge, understand 猜测	**段** (N3) grade, steps, stairs 步	**横** (N3) sideways, side, horizontal, width, woof 侧
深 (N3) deep, heighten, intensify, strengthen 深	**申** (N3) have the honor to, sign of the monkey, 3-5PM 猴	**様** (N3) Esq., way, manner, situation, polite suffix 情况	**財** (N3) property, money, wealth, assets 财富
港 (N3) harbor 港口	**識** (N3) discriminating, know, write 区分	**呼** (N3) call, call out to, invite 邀请	**達** (N3) accomplished, reach, arrive, attain 完成的
良 (N3) good, pleasing, skilled 好	**候** (N3) climate, season, weather 天气	**程** (N3) extent, degree, law, formula, distance, limits 程度	**満** (N3) full, enough, pride, satisfy 充分
敗 (N3) failure, defeat, reversal 打败	**値** (N3) price, cost, value 值	**光** (N3) ray, light 射线	**路** (N3) path, route, road, distance 路线

科 N3 department, course, section 部门	**積** N3 volume, product (x*y), acreage, contents, pile up 体积	**他** N3 other, another, the others 其他	**処** N3 dispose, manage, deal with, sentence, condemn 处置
太 N3 plump, thick, big around 厚	**客** N3 guest, visitor, customer, client 客人	**否** N3 negate, no, noes, refuse, decline, deny 否定	**師** N3 expert, teacher, master, army, war 专家
登 N3 ascend, climb up 上升	**易** N3 easy, ready to, simple, fortune-telling, divination 简单	**速** N3 quick, fast 速度	**存** N3 suppose, be aware of, believe, feel 假设
飛 N3 fly, skip (pages), scatter 飞	**殺** N3 kill, murder, butcher, slice off, split, diminish 杀	**号** N3 nickname, number, item, title, pseudonym, name, call 昵称	**単** N3 simple, one, single, merely 简单
座 N3 squat, seat, cushion, gathering, sit 座位	**破** N3 rend, rip, tear, break, destroy, defeat, frustrate 破碎	**除** N3 exclude, division (x, 3), remove, abolish, cancel 除了	**完** N3 perfect, completion, end 完善

<table>
<tr>
<td>

降 N3

descend, precipitate, fall, surrender

下降

</td>
<td>

責 N3

blame, condemn, censure

怪

</td>
<td>

捕 N3

catch, capture

抓住

</td>
<td>

危 N3

dangerous, fear, uneasy

危险的

</td>
</tr>
<tr>
<td>

給 N3

salary, wage, gift, allow, grant, bestow on

薪水

</td>
<td>

苦 N3

suffering, trial, worry, hardship, feel bitter

痛苦

</td>
<td>

迎 N3

welcome, meet, greet

欢迎

</td>
<td>

園 N3

park, garden, yard, farm

花园

</td>
</tr>
<tr>
<td>

具 N3

tool, utensil, means, possess, ingredients

用具

</td>
<td>

辞 N3

resign, word, term, expression

辞职

</td>
<td>

因 N3

cause, factor, be associated with, depend on

因为

</td>
<td>

馬 N3

horse

马

</td>
</tr>
<tr>
<td>

愛 N3

love, affection, favourite

爱

</td>
<td>

富 N3

wealth, enrich, abundant

丰富

</td>
<td>

彼 N3

he, that, the

他

</td>
<td>

未 N3

un-, not yet, hitherto, still, even now

不

</td>
</tr>
<tr>
<td>

舞 N3

dance, flit, circle, wheel

舞蹈

</td>
<td>

亡 N3

deceased, the late, dying, perish

死者

</td>
<td>

冷 N3

cool, cold (beer, person), chill

寒意

</td>
<td>

適 N3

suitable, occasional, rare, qualified, capable

适当

</td>
</tr>
</table>

N3	N3	N3	N3
婦	**寄**	**込**	**顔**
lady, woman, wife, bride	draw near, stop in, bring near, gather, collect	crowded, mixture, in bulk, included	face, expression
女人	发送	挤	表达
類	**余**	**王**	**返**
sort, kind, variety, class, genus	too much, myself, surplus, other, remainder	king, rule, magnate	return, answer, fade, repay
类	我	国王	返回
妻	**背**	**熱**	**宿**
wife, spouse	stature, height, back, behind, disobey, defy	heat, temperature, fever, mania, passion	inn, lodging, relay station, dwell, lodge
妻子	身材	热	旅店
藥	**頼**	**覚**	**船**
medicine, chemical, enamel, gunpowder, benefit	trust, request	memorize, learn, remember, awake, sober up	ship, boat
医学	信任	记住	渡船
途	**許**	**抜**	**便**
route, way, road	permit, approve	slip out, extract, pull out, pilfer, quote, remove	convenience
路线	批准	提取	方便

留 (N3)	罪 (N3)	努 (N3)	精 (N3)
detain, fasten, halt, stop	guilt, sin, crime, fault, blame, offense	toil, diligent, as much as possible	refined, ghost, fairy, energy, vitality, semen
扣留	犯罪	勤奋	精制
散 (N3)	静 (N3)	婚 (N3)	喜 (N3)
scatter, disperse, spend, squander	quiet	marriage	rejoice, take pleasure in
分散	安静	婚姻	麾
浮 (N3)	絶 (N3)	幸 (N3)	押 (N3)
floating, float, rise to surface	discontinue, beyond, sever, cut off, abstain	happiness, blessing, fortune	push, stop, check, subdue, attach
浮动	中断	幸福	推
倒 (N3)	老 (N3)	曲 (N3)	払 (N3)
overthrow, fall, collapse, drop, break down	old man, old age, grow old	bend, music, melody, composition	pay, clear out, prune, banish, dispose of
推翻	旧	音乐	工资
庭 (N3)	徒 (N3)	勤 (N3)	遅 (N3)
courtyard, garden, yard	junior, emptiness, vanity, futility, uselessness	diligence, become employed, serve	slow, late, back, later
庭院	初级	勤勉	慢

居 N3 reside, to be, exist, live with 居住	**雑** N3 miscellaneous 杂	**招** N3 beckon, invite, summon, engage 招手	**困** N3 quandary, become distressed, annoyed 懊恼
刻 N3 engrave, cut fine, chop, hash, mince, time, carving 刻	**賛** N3 approve, praise, title or inscription on picture 批准	**抱** N3 embrace, hug, hold in arms 拥抱	**犯** N3 crime, sin, offense 犯罪
恐 N3 fear, dread, awe 恐惧	**息** N3 breath, respiration, son, interest (on money) 呼吸	**遠** N3 distant, far 遥远	**戻** N3 re-, return, revert, resume, restore, go backwards 返回
願 N3 petition, request, vow, wish, hope 请愿	**絵** N3 picture, drawing, painting, sketch 图片	**越** N3 surpass, cross over, move to, exceed, Vietnam 超过	**欲** N3 longing, covetousness, greed, passion, desire 热情
痛 N3 pain, hurt, damage, bruise 疼痛	**笑** N3 laugh 笑	**互** N3 mutually, reciprocally, together 相互	**束** N3 bundle, sheaf, ream, tie in bundles, govern 束

似 N3	**列** N3	**探** N3	**逃** N3
becoming, resemble, counterfeit, imitate, suitable	file, row, rank, tier, column	grope, search, look for	escape, flee, shirk, evade, set free
类似	柱	探索	逃逸
遊 N3	**迷** N3	**夢** N3	**君** N3
play	astray, be perplexed, in doubt, lost, err, illusion	dream, vision, illusion	old boy, name-suffix
游览	误入歧途	梦想	老男孩
閉 N3	**緒** N3	**折** N3	**草** N3
closed, shut	thong, beginning, inception, end, cord, strap	fold, break, fracture, bend, yield, submit	grass, weeds, herbs, pasture, write, draft
关	开始	折	草
暮 N3	**酒** N3	**悲** N3	**晴** N3
livelihood, make a living, spend time	sake, alcohol	jail cell, grieve, sad, deplore, regret	clear up
生计	酒	伤心	明确
掛 N3	**到** N3	**寝** N3	**暗** N3
hang, suspend, depend, arrive at, tax, pour	arrival, proceed, reach, attain, result in	lie down, sleep, rest, bed, remain unsold	darkness, disappear, shade, informal
挂	到达	睡觉	黑暗

N3	N3	N3	N3
盗 steal, rob, pilfer 偷	**吸** suck, imbibe, inhale, sip 吸入	**陽** sunshine, yang principle, positive, male, heaven 阳光	**御** honorable, manipulate, govern 光荣的
歯 tooth, cog 齿	**忘** forget 忘记	**雪** snow 雪	**吹** blow, breathe, puff, emit, smoke 吹
娘 daughter, girl 女儿	**誤** mistake, err, do wrong, mislead 错误	**洗** wash, inquire into, probe 洗	**慣** accustomed, get used to, become experienced 习惯的
礼 salute, bow, ceremony, thanks, remuneration 仪式	**窓** window, pane 窗口	**昔** once upon a time, antiquity, old times 古代	**貧** poverty, poor 贫穷
怒 angry, be offended 愤怒	**泳** swim 游泳的	**祖** ancestor, pioneer, founder 祖先	**杯** counter for cupfuls, wine glass, glass, toast 杯子

疲 N3 exhausted, tire, weary 累	**皆** N3 all, everything 一切	**腹** N3 abdomen, belly, stomach 肚皮	**煙** N3 smoke 抽烟
眠 N3 sleep, die, sleepy 睡觉	**怖** N3 dreadful, be frightened, fearful 恐怖	**耳** N3 ear 耳	**頂** N3 place on the head, receive, top of head, top, summit 最佳
箱 N3 box, chest, case, bin, railway car 框	**晩** N3 nightfall, night 黄昏	**寒** N3 cold 冷	**髪** N3 hair of the head 头发
忙 N3 busy, occupied, restless 忙	**才** N3 genius, years old, cubic shaku 天才	**靴** N3 shoes 鞋子	**恥** N3 shame, dishonor 耻辱
偶 N3 accidentally, even number, couple, man & wife 偶然	**偉** N3 admirable, greatness, remarkable, conceited 令人钦佩的	**猫** N3 cat 猫	**幾** N3 how many, how much, how far, how long 多少

Kanji	Meaning	Example
党 (N2)	party, faction, clique	派対
協 (N2)	co-, cooperation	合作
総 (N2)	general, whole, all, full, total	一般
区 (N2)	ward, district	区
領 (N2)	jurisdiction, dominion, territory, fief, reign	统治权
県 (N2)	prefecture	州
設 (N2)	establishment, provision, prepare	建立
改 (N2)	reformation, change, modify, mend, renew	改革
府 (N2)	borough, urban prefecture, govt office	屋
査 (N2)	investigate	调查
委 (N2)	committee, entrust to, leave to, devote, discard	委员会
軍 (N2)	army, force, troops, war, battle	军事
団 (N2)	group, association	组
各 (N2)	each, every, either	每
島 (N2)	island	岛
革 (N2)	leather, become serious, skin, hide, pelt	皮革
村 (N2)	town, village	村
勢 (N2)	forces, energy, military strength	力量
減 (N2)	dwindle, decrease, reduce, decline, curtail	减少
再 (N2)	again, twice, second time	再次

税 N2	営 N2	比 N2	防 N2
tax, duty	occupation, camp, perform, build, conduct (business)	compare, race, ratio, Philipines	ward off, defend, protect, resist
税	占用	比较	保护
補 N2	境 N2	導 N2	副 N2
supplement, supply, make good, offset, compensate	boundary, border, region	guidance, leading, conduct, usher	vice-, duplicate, copy
补充	边界	指导	重复
算 N2	輸 N2	述 N2	線 N2
calculate, divining, number, abacus, probability	transport, send, be inferior	mention, state, speak, relate	line, track
计算	运输	提到	线
農 N2	州 N2	武 N2	象 N2
agriculture, farmers	state, province	warrior, military, chivalry, arms	elephant, pattern after, imitate, image, shape
农业	省	战士	象
域 N2	額 N2	欧 N2	担 N2
range, region, limits, stage, level	forehead, tablet, plaque, framed picture, sum	Europe	shouldering, carry, raise, bear
区域	前额	欧洲	肩负

準 — N2 semi-, correspond to, proportionate to, conform 符合	**賞** — N2 prize, reward, praise 奖励	**辺** — N2 environs, boundary, border, vicinity 边界	**造** — N2 create, make, structure, physique 创建
被 — N2 incur, cover, veil, brood over, shelter, wear 招致	**技** — N2 skill, art, craft, ability, feat, performance 技能	**低** — N2 lower, short, humble 低	**復** — N2 restore, return to, revert, resume 恢复
移 — N2 shift, move, change, drift, catch (cold, fire) 转移	**個** — N2 individual, counter for articles and military units 个人	**門** — N2 gates 盖茨	**課** — N2 chapter, lesson, section, department, division 课
脳 — N2 brain, memory 脑	**極** — N2 poles, settlement, conclusion, end 极	**含** — N2 include, bear in mind, understand, cherish 包括	**蔵** — N2 storehouse, hide, own, have, possess 库
量 — N2 quantity, measure, weight, amount, consider 数量	**型** — N2 mould, type, model 模子	**況** — N2 condition, situation 条件	**針** — N2 needle, pin, staple, stinger 针

専 N2 specialty, exclusive, mainly, solely 专业	**谷** N2 valley 谷	**史** N2 history, chronicle 历史	**階** N2 storey, stair, counter for storeys of a building 层
管 N2 pipe, tube, wind instrument, drunken talk 管	**兵** N2 soldier, private, troops, army, warfare, strategy 士兵	**接** N2 touch, contact, adjoin, piece together 触摸	**細** N2 dainty, get thin, taper, slender, narrow 精致的
劾 N2 merit, efficacy, efficiency, benefit 值得	**丸** N2 round, full, month, perfection, -ship, pills 回合	**湾** N2 gulf, bay, inlet 湾	**録** N2 record 记录
省 N2 focus, government ministry, conserve 焦点	**橋** N2 bridge 桥	**岸** N2 beach 岸	**周** N2 circumference, circuit, lap 周
材 N2 lumber, log, timber, wood, talent 木材	**戸** N2 door 门	**央** N2 center, middle 中央	**券** N2 ticket 票

編 N2	搜 N2	竹 N2	並 N2
compilation, knit, plait, braid, twist, editing	search, look for, locate	bamboo	row, and, besides, as well as, line up, rank with
汇编	搜索	竹	除了
療 N2	採 N2	森 N2	競 N2
heal, cure	pick, take, fetch, take up	forest, woods	emulate, compete with, bid, sell at auction
愈合	挑	森林	仿真
介 N2	根 N2	販 N2	歴 N2
jammed in, shellfish, mediate, concern oneself with	root, radical, head (pimple)	marketing, sell, trade	curriculum, continuation, passage of time
贝类	根	行销	课程
将 N2	幅 N2	般 N2	貿 N2
leader, commander, general, admiral, or	hanging scroll, width	carrier, carry, all	trade, exchange
领导	宽度	载体	贸易
講 N2	林 N2	装 N2	諸 N2
lecture, club, association	grove, forest	attire, dress, pretend, disguise, profess	various, many, several, together
演讲	森林	服装	各种

劇 N2	河 N2	航 N2	鉄 N2
drama, play	river	navigate, sail, cruise, fly	iron
戏剧	河	导航	铁
児 N2	禁 N2	印 N2	逆 N2
newborn babe, child, young of animals	prohibition, ban, forbid	stamp, seal, mark, imprint, symbol, emblem	inverted, reverse, opposite, wicked
小儿科	禁令	密封	逆
換 N2	久 N2	短 N2	油 N2
interchange, period, charge, change?	long time, old story	short, brevity, fault, defect, weak point	oil, fat
更改	很久	简洁	油
暴 N2	輪 N2	占 N2	植 N2
outburst, rave, fret, force, violence, cruelty	wheel, ring, circle, link, loop	fortune-telling, divining, forecasting, occupy	plant
暴力	轮	算命	厂
清 N2	倍 N2	均 N2	億 N2
pure, purify, cleanse, exorcise, Manchu dynasty	double, twice, times, fold	level, average	hundred million
纯	双	水平	十亿

圧 (N2)	芸 (N2)	署 (N2)	伸 (N2)
pressure, push, overwhelm, oppress, dominate	technique, art, craft, performance, acting	signature, govt office, police station	expand, stretch, extend, lengthen, increase
压力	技术	签名	伸展
停 (N2)	爆 (N2)	陸 (N2)	玉 (N2)
halt, stopping	bomb, burst open, pop, split	land, six	jewel, ball
停止	爆	土地	宝石
波 (N2)	帯 (N2)	延 (N2)	羽 (N2)
waves, billows, Poland	sash, belt, obi, zone, region	prolong, stretching	feathers, counter for birds, rabbits
波	窗扇	延长	羽毛
固 (N2)	則 (N2)	乱 (N2)	普 (N2)
harden, set, clot, curdle	rule, follow, based on, model after	riot, war, disorder, disturb	universal, wide(ly), generally, Prussia
固体	规则	紊乱	一般
測 (N2)	豊 (N2)	厚 (N2)	齢 (N2)
fathom, plan, scheme, measure	bountiful, excellent, rich	thick, heavy, rich, kind, cordial, brazen, shameless	age
方案	优秀	厚	年龄

N2	N2	N2	N2
囲	**卒**	**略**	**承**
surround, besiege, store, paling, enclosure	graduate, soldier, private, die	abbreviation, omission, outline, shorten, capture	acquiesce, hear, listen to, be informed, receive
环绕	毕业	缩写	默许
N2	N2	N2	N2
順	**岩**	**練**	**軽**
obey, order, turn, right, docility, occasion	boulder, rock, cliff	practice, gloss, train, drill, polish, refine	lightly, trifling, unimportant
遵守	岩石	实践	轻轻
N2	N2	N2	N2
了	**庁**	**城**	**患**
complete, finish	government office	castle	afflicted, disease, suffer from, be ill
完	政府办公室	城堡	遭受
N2	N2	N2	N2
層	**版**	**令**	**角**
stratum, social class, layer, story, floor	printing block, printing plate, edition, impression	orders, ancient laws, command, decree	angle, corner, square, horn, antlers
层	标签	命令	角度
N2	N2	N2	N2
絡	**損**	**募**	**裏**
entwine, coil around, get caught in	damage, loss, disadvantage, hurt, injure	recruit, campaign, gather (contributions)	back, amidst, in, reverse, inside, palm, sole
缠绕	损伤	招	之中

N2	N2	N2	N2
仏	績	築	貨
Buddha, the dead, France	exploits, unreeling cocoons	fabricate, build, construct	freight, goods, property
佛	漏洞利用	制造	货物
N2	N2	N2	N2
混	昇	池	血
mix, blend, confuse	rise up	pond, cistern, pool, reservoir	blood
混合	上升	泳池	血液
N2	N2	N2	N2
温	季	星	永
warm	seasons	star, spot, dot, mark	eternity, long, lengthy
暖	季节	星	永远
N2	N2	N2	N2
著	誌	庫	刊
renowned, publish, write, remarkable	document, records	warehouse, storehouse	publish, carve, engrave
著名的	文献	仓库	发布
N2	N2	N2	N2
像	香	坂	底
statue, picture, image, figure, portrait	incense, smell, perfume	slope, incline, hill	bottom, sole, depth, bottom price, base, kind, sort
图片	香	坡	底部

布 N2 linen, cloth 布	**寺** N2 Buddhist temple 寺庙	**宇** N2 eaves, roof, house, heaven 屋顶	**巨** N2 gigantic, big, large, great 巨大
震 N2 quake, shake, tremble, quiver, shiver 颤抖	**希** N2 hope, beg, request, pray, beseech, Greece 希望	**触** N2 contact, touch, feel, hit, proclaim, announce 触摸	**依** N2 reliant, depend on, consequently, therefore, due to 根据
籍 N2 enroll, domiciliary register, membership 注册	**汚** N2 dirty, pollute, disgrace, rape, defile 脏	**枚** N2 sheet of..., counter for flat thin objects or sheets 床单	**複** N2 duplicate, double, compound, multiple 复杂
郵 N2 mail, stagecoach stop 邮件	**仲** N2 go-between, relationship 关系	**栄** N2 flourish, prosperity, honor, glory, splendor 繁荣	**札** N2 tag, paper money, counter for bonds, placard, bid 标签
板 N2 plank, board, plate, stage 板	**骨** N2 skeleton, bone, remains, frame 骨	**傾** N2 lean, incline, tilt, trend, wane, sink, ruin, bias 倾	**届** N2 deliver, reach, arrive, report, notify, forward 交付

N2	N2	N2	N2
卷	燃	跡	包
scroll, volume, book, part, roll up	burn, blaze, glow	tracks, mark, print, impression	wrap, pack up, cover, conceal
体积	烧伤	跟踪	包

N2	N2	N2	N2
駐	弱	紹	雇
stop-over, reside in, resident	weak, frail	introduce, inherit, help	employ, hire
站	弱	介绍	聘请

N2	N2	N2	N2
替	預	焼	簡
exchange, spare, substitute, per-	deposit, custody, leave with, entrust to	bake, burning	simplicity, brevity
交换	存款	烘烤	简单

N2	N2	N2	N2
章	臟	律	贈
badge, chapter, composition, poem, design	entrails, viscera, bowels	rhythm, law, regulation, gauge, control	presents, send, give to, award to, confer on
徽章	内脏	韵律	礼物

N2	N2	N2	N2
照	薄	群	奥
illuminate, shine, compare, bashful	dilute, thin, weak (tea)	flock, group, crowd, herd, swarm, cluster	heart, interior
闪耀	瘦	组	心

詰

packed, close, pressed, reprove, rebuke, blame

骂

双

pair, set, comparison, counter for pairs

双

刺

thorn, pierce, stab, prick, sting, calling card

刺

純

genuine, purity, innocence, net (profit)

纯

翌

the following, next

下一个

快

cheerful, pleasant, agreeable, comfortable

愉快

片

one-sided, leaf, sheet

叶

敬

awe, respect, honor, revere

尊敬

悩

trouble, worry, in pain, distress, illness

麻烦

泉

spring, fountain

弹簧

皮

pelt, skin, hide, leather

皮肤

漁

fishing, fishery

钓鱼

荒

laid waste, rough, rude, wild

无礼

貯

savings, store, lay in, keep, wear mustache

储蓄

硬

stiff, hard

硬

埋

bury, be filled up, embedded

埋葬

柱

pillar, post, cylinder, support

柱

祭

ritual, offer prayers, celebrate, deify

仪式

袋

sack, bag, pouch

袋

筆

writing brush, writing, painting brush, handwriting

画笔

訓 N2	浴 N2	童 N2	宝 N2
instruction, Japanese character reading	bathe, be favored with, bask in	juvenile, child	treasure, wealth, valuables
指令	浴	儿童	宝藏
封 N2	胸 N2	砂 N2	塩 N2
seal, closing	bosom, breast, chest, heart, feelings	sand	salt
密封	乳房	砂	盐
賢 N2	腕 N2	兆 N2	床 N2
intelligent, wise, wisdom, cleverness	arm, ability, talent	portent, 10**12, trillion, sign, omen, symptoms	bed, floor, padding, tatami
智能	腕	兆	床
毛 N2	緑 N2	尊 N2	祝 N2
fur, hair, feather, down	green	revered, valuable, precious, noble, exalted	celebrate, congratulate
头发	绿色	有价值	庆祝
柔 N2	殿 N2	濃 N2	液 N2
tender, weakness, gentleness, softness	Mr., hall, mansion, palace, temple, lord	concentrated, thick, dark, undiluted	fluid, liquid, juice, sap, secretion
投标	寺庙	集中	液体

N2 衣	N2 肩	N2 零	N2 幼
garment, clothes, dressing	shoulder	zero, spill, overflow, nothing, cipher	infancy, childhood
衣服	肩	零	童年
N2 荷	N2 泊	N2 黄	N2 甘
baggage, shoulder-pole load	overnight, put up at, ride at anchor, 3-day stay	yellow	sweet, coax, pamper, be content, sugary
行李	过夜	黄色	甜
N2 臣	N2 浅	N2 掃	N2 雲
retainer, subject	shallow, superficial, frivolous, wretched, shameful	sweep, brush	cloud
固定器	浅	扫	云
N2 掘	N2 捨	N2 軟	N2 沈
dig, delve, excavate	discard, throw away, abandon, resign, reject	soft	sink, be submerged, subside, be depressed, aloes
挖	丢弃	柔软的	下沉
N2 凍	N2 乳	N2 恋	N2 紅
frozen, congeal, refrigerate	milk, breasts	romance, in love, yearn for, miss, darling	crimson, deep red
冻结	牛奶	爱	红色

N2	N2	N2	N2
郊	腰	炭	踊
outskirts, suburbs, rural area	loins, hips, waist, low wainscoting	charcoal, coal	jump, dance, leap, skip
市郊	腰部	碳	飞跃

N2	N2	N2	N2
冊	勇	械	菜
tome, counter for books, volume	courage, cheer up, be in high spirits, bravery	contraption, fetter, machine, instrument	vegetable, side dish, greens
对我来说	勇敢	仪器	蔬菜

N2	N2	N2	N2
珍	卵	湖	喫
rare, curious, strange	egg, ovum, spawn, roe	lake	consume, eat, drink, smoke, receive (a blow)
好奇	蛋	湖	吃

N2	N2	N2	N2
干	虫	刷	湯
dry, parch	insect, bug, temper	printing, print	hot water, bath, hot spring
干	昆虫	刷	热水

N2	N2	N2	N2
溶	鉱	涙	匹
melt, dissolve, thaw	mineral, ore	tears, sympathy	equal, head, counter for small animals
溶解	矿物	眼泪	等于

Kanji	Meaning	Example
孫 (N2)	grandchild, descendants	孙子
鋭 (N2)	pointed, sharpness, edge, weapon, sharp, violent	锐度
枝 (N2)	bough, branch, twig, limb	树枝
塗 (N2)	paint, plaster, daub, smear, coating	绘
軒 (N2)	flats, counter for houses, eaves	公寓
毒 (N2)	poison, virus, venom, germ, harm, injury, spite	毒
叫 (N2)	shout, exclaim, yell	喊
拝 (N2)	worship, adore, pray to	崇拜
氷 (N2)	icicle, ice, hail, freeze, congeal	冰柱
乾 (N2)	drought, dry, dessicate, drink up, heaven, emperor	干旱
棒 (N2)	rod, stick, cane, pole, club, line	竿
祈 (N2)	pray, wish	祈祷
拾 (N2)	pick up, gather, find, go on foot, ten	收集
粉 (N2)	flour, powder, dust	粉末
糸 (N2)	thread	线
綿 (N2)	cotton	棉
汗 (N2)	sweat, perspire	流汗
銅 (N2)	copper	铜
湿 (N2)	damp, wet, moist	湿
瓶 (N2)	flower pot, bottle, vial, jar, jug, vat, urn	瓶子

N2	N2	N2	N2
咲	**召**	**缶**	**隻**
blossom, bloom	seduce, call, send for, wear, put on, ride in	tin can, container	vessels, counter for ships, fish, birds, arrows
开花	勾引	陶器	船只
脂	**蒸**	**肌**	**耕**
fat, grease, tallow, lard, rosin, gum, tar	steam, heat, sultry, foment, get musty	texture, skin, body, grain	till, plow, cultivate
润滑脂	蒸汽	肌肉	犁
钝	**泥**	**隅**	**灯**
dull, slow, foolish, blunt	mud, mire, adhere to, be attached to	corner, nook	lamp, a light, light, counter for lights
钝	泥	角	灯
辛	**磨**	**麦**	**姓**
spicy, bitter, hot, acrid	grind, polish, scour, improve, brush (teeth)	barley, wheat	surname
辣的	研磨	小麦	姓
筒	**鼻**	**粒**	**詞**
cylinder, pipe, tube, gun barrel, sleeve	nose, snout	grains, drop, counter for tiny particles	part of speech, words, poetry
圆筒	鼻子	粮食	诗歌

胃 — N2 stomach, paunch, crop, craw 胃	**畳** — N2 tatami mat, counter for tatami mats, fold 折	**机** — N2 desk, table 台	**膚** — N2 skin, body, grain, texture, disposition 皮肤
濯 — N2 laundry, wash, pour on, rinse 洗衣房	**塔** — N2 pagoda, tower, steeple 塔	**沸** — N2 seethe, boil, ferment, uproar, breed 沸腾	**灰** — N2 ashes, puckery juice, cremate 灰烬
菓 — N2 candy, cakes, fruit 糖果	**帽** — N2 cap, headgear 帽	**枯** — N2 wither, die, dry up, be seasoned 干枯	**涼** — N2 refreshing, nice and cool 令人耳目一新
舟 — N2 boat, ship 船	**貝** — N2 shellfish 贝类	**符** — N2 token, sign, mark, tally, charm 符号	**憎** — N2 hate, detest 讨厌
皿 — N2 dish, a helping, plate 碟	**肯** — N2 agreement, consent, comply with 协议	**燥** — N2 parch, dry up 干	**畜** — N2 livestock, domestic fowl and animals 家畜

挟 N2	曇 N2	滴 N2	伺 N2
pinch, between	cloudy weather, cloud up	drip, drop	pay respects, visit, ask, inquire, question, implore
捏	多云的	下降	尊重
氏 N2	統 N2	保 N2	第 N2
family name, surname, clan	overall, relationship, ruling, governing	protect, guarantee, keep, preserve, sustain, support	No., residence
姓	总体	保护	住宅
結 N2	派 N2	案 N2	策 N2
tie, bind, contract, join, organize, do up hair	faction, group, party, clique, sect, school	plan, suggestion, draft, ponder, fear, proposition	scheme, plan, policy, step, means
合同	派	建议	政策
基 N2	価 N2	提 N2	挙 N2
fundamentals, radical (chem), counter for machines	value, price	propose, take along, carry in hand	raise, plan, project, behavior, actions
基本面	值	提出	提高
応 N2	企 N2	検 N2	沢 N2
apply, answer, yes, OK, reply, accept	undertake, scheme, design, attempt, plan	examination, investigate	swamp
应用	承担	检查	沼泽

N1	N1	N1	N1
裁 tailor, judge, decision, cut out (pattern) 裁缝	**証** evidence, proof, certificate 证书	**援** abet, help, save 援助	**施** alms, apply bandages, administer first-aid 施舍
井 well, well crib, town, community 好	**護** safeguard, protect 保护	**展** unfold, expand 展开	**態** attitude, condition, figure, appearance 态度
鮮 fresh, vivid, clear, brilliant, Korea 新鲜	**視** inspection, regard as, see, look at 检查	**条** article, clause, item, stripe, streak 文章	**幹** tree trunk 树干
独 single, alone, spontaneously, Germany 单独	**宮** Shinto shrine, constellations, palace, princess 星座	**率** ratio, rate, proportion, %, coefficient, factor 比	**衛** defense, protection 防御
張 lengthen, counter for bows & stringed instruments 加长	**監** oversee, official, govt office, rule, administer 监督	**環** ring, circle, link, wheel 圈	**審** hearing, judge, trial 评论

N1	N1	N1	N1
義	**訴**	**株**	**姿**
righteousness, justice, morality, honor, loyalty	accusation, sue, complain of pain, appeal to	stocks, stump, shares, stock	figure, form, shape
义	抱怨	树桩	姿势

N1	N1	N1	N1
閣	**衆**	**評**	**影**
tower, tall building, palace	masses, great numbers, multitude, populace	evaluate, criticism, comment	shadow, silhouette, phantom
塔	群众	评估	阴影

N1	N1	N1	N1
松	**撃**	**佐**	**核**
pine tree	beat, attack, defeat, conquer	assistant, help	nucleus, core, kernel
松树	击败	助理	核

N1	N1	N1	N1
整	**融**	**製**	**票**
organize, arranging, tune, tone, meter, key (music)	dissolve, melt	made in..., manufacture	ballot, label, ticket, sign
组织	熔化	制造	选票

N1	N1	N1	N1
渉	**響**	**推**	**請**
ford, ferry, port	echo, also N5116, sound, resound, ring, vibrate	conjecture, infer, guess, suppose, support	solicit, invite, ask
渡船	回声	推测	请

器 (N1)	士 (N1)	討 (N1)	攻 (N1)
utensil, vessel, receptacle, implement, instrument	gentleman, samurai	chastise, attack, defeat, destroy, conquer	aggression, attack
用具	绅士	惩戒	攻击
崎 (N1)	督 (N1)	授 (N1)	催 (N1)
promontory, cape, spit	coach, command, urge, lead, supervise	impart, instruct, grant, confer	sponsor, hold (a meeting), give (a dinner)
海角	教练	格兰特	赞助
及 (N1)	憲 (N1)	摘 (N1)	系 (N1)
reach out, exert, exercise, cause	constitution, law	pinch, pick, pluck, trim, clip, summarize	lineage, system
发挥	宪法	挑	血统
批 (N1)	郎 (N1)	健 (N1)	盟 (N1)
criticism, strike	son, counter for sons	healthy, health, strength, persistence	alliance, oath
批评	儿子	健康	联盟
従 (N1)	修 (N1)	隊 (N1)	織 (N1)
accompany, obey, submit to, comply, follow	discipline, conduct oneself well, study, master	regiment, party, company, squad	weave, fabric
陪	学科	团	编织

拡 (N1) broaden, extend, expand, enlarge 扩大	**故** (N1) happenstance, especially 偶然	**振** (N1) shake, wave, wag, swing 抖动	**弁** (N1) valve, petal, braid, speech, dialect, discrimination 阀
就 (N1) concerning, settle, take position, depart 关于	**異** (N1) uncommon, queerness, strangeness, wonderful 罕见	**献** (N1) offering, counter for drinks, present, offer 提供	**厳** (N1) stern, strictness, severity, rigidity 船尾
維 (N1) fiber, tie, rope 纤维	**浜** (N1) seacoast, beach, seashore 海滩	**遺** (N1) bequeath, leave behind, reserve 遗赠	**塁** (N1) bases, fort, rampart, walls, base(ball) 基地
邦 (N1) home country, country, Japan 国家	**素** (N1) elementary, principle, naked, uncovered 初级	**遣** (N1) despatch, send, give, donate, do, undertake 寄发	**抗** (N1) confront, resist, defy, oppose 面对
模 (N1) imitation, copy, mock 仿制	**雄** (N1) masculine, male, hero, leader, superiority 男性	**益** (N1) benefit, gain, profit, advantage 有利	**緊** (N1) tense, solid, hard, reliable, tight 紧

N1	N1	N1	N1
標	**宣**	**昭**	**廃**
signpost, seal, mark, stamp, imprint	proclaim, say, announce	shining, bright	abolish, obsolete, cessation, discarding, abandon
密封	宣布	亮	廃除
N1	N1	N1	N1
伊	**江**	**僚**	**吉**
Italy, that one	creek, inlet, bay	colleague, official, companion	good luck, joy, congratulations
意大利	溪	同事	恭喜
N1	N1	N1	N1
皇	**臨**	**踏**	**壊**
emperor	look to, face, meet, confront, attend, call on	step, trample, carry through, appraise	demolition, break, destroy
皇帝	面对	践踏	拆除
N1	N1	N1	N1
債	**興**	**源**	**儀**
bond, loan, debt	entertain, revive, retrieve, interest, pleasure	source, origin	ceremony, rule, affair, case, a matter
债务	招待	资源	仪式
N1	N1	N1	N1
創	**障**	**継**	**筋**
genesis, wound, injury, hurt, start, originate	hinder, hurt, harm	inherit, succeed, patch, graft (tree)	muscle, sinew, tendon, fiber, plot, plan, descent
成因	阻碍	继承	肌肉

闘 N1 fight, war 斗争	**葬** N1 interment, bury, shelve 情趣	**避** N1 evade, avoid, avert, ward off, shirk, shun 避免	**司** N1 director, official, govt office, rule, administer 导向器
康 N1 ease, peace 缓解	**善** N1 virtuous, good, goodness 好	**逮** N1 apprehend, chase 理解	**迫** N1 urge, force, imminent, spur on 力
惑 N1 beguile, delusion, perplexity 幻想	**崩** N1 crumble, die, demolish, level 崩溃	**紀** N1 chronicle, account, narrative, history, annals 编年史	**聴** N1 listen, headstrong, naughty, careful inquiry 听
脱 N1 undress, removing, escape from, get rid of 脱衣服	**級** N1 class, rank, grade 水平	**博** N1 Dr., command, esteem, win acclaim, Ph.D., 尊重	**締** N1 tighten, tie, shut, lock, fasten 紧缩
救 N1 salvation, save, help, rescue, reclaim 保存	**執** N1 tenacious, take hold, grasp, take to heart 顽强	**房** N1 tassel, tuft, fringe, bunch, lock (hair) 条纹	**撤** N1 remove, withdraw, disarm, dismantle, reject, exclude 退出

N1	N1	N1	N1
削	**密**	**措**	**志**
plane, sharpen, whittle, pare	secrecy, density (pop), minuteness, carefulness	set aside, give up, suspend, discontinue, lay aside	intention, plan, resolve, aspire, motive, hopes
锐化	保密	暂停	意向
載	**陣**	**我**	**為**
ride, board, get on, place, spread, 10**44	camp, battle array, ranks, position	ego, I, selfish, our, oneself	do, change, make, benefit
骑	营	自我	效益
抑	**幕**	**染**	**奈**
repress, well, now, in the first place, push	curtain, bunting, act of play	dye, color, paint, stain, print	Nara, what?
压制	窗帘	染料	什么
傷	**択**	**秀**	**徵**
wound, hurt, injure, impair, pain, injury, cut	choose, select, elect, prefer	excel, excellence, beauty, surpass	indications, sign, omen, symptom, collect, seek
伤害	选择	卓越	适应症
弾	**償**	**功**	**拠**
bullet, twang, flip, snap	reparation, make up for, recompense, redeem	achievement, merits, success, honor, credit	foothold, based on, follow, therefore
子弹	赔偿	成就	立足点

N1	N1	N1	N1
秘	**拒**	**刑**	**塚**
secret, conceal	repel, refuse, reject, decline	punish, penalty, sentence, punishment	hillock, mound
秘密	垃圾	惩罚	冢
N1	N1	N1	N1
致	**繰**	**尾**	**描**
doth, do, send, forward, cause, exert, incur, engage	winding, reel, spin, turn (pages), look up, refer to	tail, end, counter for fish, lower slope of mountain	sketch, compose, write, draw, paint
向前	卷轴	尾巴	草图
N1	N1	N1	N1
鈴	**盤**	**項**	**喪**
small bell, buzzer	tray, shallow bowl, platter, tub, board	paragraph, nape of neck, clause, item	miss, mourning
钟	托盘	段	丧
N1	N1	N1	N1
伴	**養**	**懸**	**街**
consort, accompany, bring with, companion	foster, bring up, rear, develop, nurture	suspend, hang, 10%, install, depend, consult	boulevard, street, town
伴侣	培育	暂停	街
N1	N1	N1	N1
契	**揭**	**躍**	**棄**
pledge, promise, vow	put up (a notice), put up, hoist, display	leap, dance, skip	abandon, throw away, discard, resign, reject
保证	提升	跳	弃

邸 N1	縮 N1	還 N1	属 N1
residence, mansion	shrink, contract, shrivel, wrinkle, reduce	send back, return	belong, genus, subordinate official, affiliated
住宅	收缩	返回	属于
慮 N1	枠 N1	惠 N1	露 N1
prudence, thought, concern, consider, deliberate	frame, framework, spindle, spool	favor, blessing, grace, kindness	dew, tears, expose, Russia
考虑	构架	宠爱	露
節 N1	需 N1	射 N1	購 N1
, clause, stanza, honor, joint, knuckle, knob, knot	demand, request, need	shoot, shine into, onto, archery	subscription, buy
期	需求	射击	采购
揮 N1	充 N1	貢 N1	鹿 N1
brandish, wave, wag, swing, shake	allot, fill	tribute, support, finance	deer
波	分配	贡	鹿
却 N1	端 N1	賃 N1	獲 N1
instead, on the contrary, rather	edge, origin, end, point, border, verge, cape	fare, fee, hire, rent, wages, charge	seize, get, find, earn, acquire, can, may, able to
但	结束	出租	获得

郡 N1 county, district 县	**併** N1 join, get together, unite, collective 加入	**徹** N1 penetrate, clear, pierce, strike home 穿透	**貴** N1 precious, value, prize, esteem, honor 珍贵
衝 N1 collide, brunt, highway, opposition (astronomy) 碰撞	**焦** N1 char, hurry, impatient, irritate, burn, scorch 匆忙	**奪** N1 rob, take by force, snatch away, dispossess, plunder 抢	**災** N1 disaster, calamity, woe, curse, evil 灾害
浦 N1 bay, creek, inlet, gulf, beach, seacoast 湾	**析** N1 chop, divide, tear, analyze 劈	**讓** N1 defer, turnover, transfer, convey 周转	**称** N1 appellation, praise, admire, name, title, fame 称谓
納 N1 settlement, obtain, reap, pay, supply, store 沉降	**樹** N1 timber trees, wood 木	**挑** N1 challenge, contend for, make love to 挑战	**誘** N1 entice, lead, tempt, invite, ask, call for 诱惑
紛 N1 distract, be mistaken for, go astray, divert 转移	**至** N1 climax, arrive, proceed, reach, attain, result in 高潮	**宗** N1 religion, sect, denomination, main point, origin 宗教	**促** N1 stimulate, urge, press, demand, incite 刺激

慎 N1 humility, be careful, discrete, prudent 谦逊	**控** N1 withdraw, draw in, hold back, refrain from 退出	**智** N1 wisdom, intellect, reason 智慧	**握** N1 grip, hold, mould sushi, bribe 握
宙 N1 mid-air, air, space, sky, memorization 宇宙	**俊** N1 sagacious, genius, excellence 明智	**銭** N1 coin, .01 yen, money 钱	**渋** N1 astringent, hesitate, reluctant, have diarrhea 犹豫
銃 N1 gun, arms 手枪	**操** N1 maneuver, manipulate, operate, steer, chastity 操纵	**携** N1 portable, carry (in hand), armed with, bring along 携带	**診** N1 checkup, seeing, diagnose, examine 检查
託 N1 consign, requesting, entrusting with, pretend, hint 交付	**撮** N1 snapshot, take pictures 快照	**誕** N1 nativity, be born, declension, lie, be arbitrary 诞生	**侵** N1 encroach, invade, raid, trespass, violate 侵犯
括 N1 fasten, tie up, arrest, constrict 系	**謝** N1 apologize, thank, refuse 道歉	**駆** N1 drive, run, gallop, advance, inspire, impel 驾驶	**透** N1 transparent, permeate, filter, penetrate 透明

津 N1 haven, port, harbor, ferry 港口	**壁** N1 wall, lining (stomach), fence 壁	**稲** N1 rice plant 水稻植物	**仮** N1 sham, temporary, interim, assumed (name), informal 临时
裂 N1 split, rend, tear 裂纹	**敏** N1 cleverness, agile, alert 机灵	**是** N1 just so, this, right, justice 正义	**排** N1 repudiate, exclude, expel, reject 否认
裕 N1 abundant, rich, fertile 丰富	**堅** N1 strict, hard, solid, tough, tight, reliable 严格	**訳** N1 translate, reason, circumstance, case 翻译	**芝** N1 turf, lawn 草坪
綱 N1 hawser, class (genus), rope, cord, cable 绳	**典** N1 code, ceremony, law, rule 码	**賀** N1 congratulations, joy 祝贺	**扱** N1 handle, entertain, thresh, strip 处理
顧 N1 look back, review, examine oneself, turn around 评论	**弘** N1 vast, broad, wide 宽	**看** N1 watch over, see 看到	**訟** N1 sue, accuse 控诉

N1	N1	N1	N1
戒	祉	誉	歓
commandment	welfare, happiness	reputation, praise, honor, glory	delight, joy
诫命	福利	声誉	喜
奏	勧	騒	閥
play music, speak to a ruler, complete	persuade, recommend, advise, encourage, offer	boisterous, make noise, clamor, disturb, excite	clique, lineage, pedigree, faction, clan
玩	说服	普遍	集团
甲	縄	郷	揺
armor, high (voice), A grade, first class, former	straw rope, cord	home town, village, native place, district	swing, shake, sway, rock, tremble, vibrate
盔甲	脐带	村	摇摆
免	既	薦	隣
excuse, dismissal	previously, already, long ago	recommend, mat, advise, encourage, offer	neighboring
借口	先前	推荐	邻接
華	範	隠	德
splendor, flower, petal, shine, luster, ostentatious	pattern, example, model	conceal, hide, cover	benevolence, virtue, goodness, commanding respect
辉煌	图案	隐藏	善良

哲 N1 philosophy, clear 哲学	**杉** N1 cedar, cryptomeria 雪松	**釈** N1 explanation 说明	**己** N1 self, snake, serpent 蛇
妥 N1 gentle, peace, depravity 温和	**威** N1 intimidate, dignity, majesty, menace, threaten 声望	**豪** N1 overpowering, great, powerful, excelling, Australia 压倒性	**熊** N1 bear 熊
滞 N1 stagnate, be delayed, overdue, arrears 停滞	**微** N1 delicate, minuteness, insignificance 细腻的	**隆** N1 hump, high, noble, prosperity 驼峰	**症** N1 symptoms, illness 症状
暫 N1 temporarily, a while, moment, long time 暂时	**忠** N1 loyalty, fidelity, faithfulness 忠诚	**倉** N1 godown, warehouse, storehouse, cellar, treasury 仓库	**彦** N1 lad, boy (ancient) 男孩
肝 N1 liver, pluck, nerve, chutzpah 肝	**喚** N1 yell, cry, scream 哭	**沿** N1 run alongside, follow along, run along, lie along 沿	**妙** N1 exquisite, strange, queer, mystery, miracle 精彩

N1	N1	N1	N1
唱 chant, recite, call upon, yell 呗	阿 Africa, flatter, fawn upon, corner, nook, recess 非洲	索 cord, rope 绳	誠 sincerity, admonish, warn, prohibit, truth 诚意
襲 attack, advance on, succeed to, pile, heap 攻击	懇 sociable, kind, courteous, hospitable, cordial 善于交际	俳 haiku, actor 演员	柄 design, pattern, build, nature, handle, crank 设计
驚 wonder, be surprised, frightened, amazed 奇迹	麻 hemp, flax 麻	李 plum 李子	浩 wide expanse, abundance, vigorous 丰富
剤 dose, medicine, drug 医学	瀬 rapids, current, torrent, shallows, shoal 当前	趣 gist, proceed to, tend, become 成为	陥 collapse, fall into, cave in, fall (castle) 坍方
斎 purification, Buddhist food, room, worship, avoid 纯化	貫 pierce, 8 1, 3lbs, penetrate, brace 刺穿	仙 hermit, wizard, cent 隐士	慰 consolation, amusement, seduce, cheer, console 安慰

序 N1 preface, beginning, order, precedence, occasion 前言	**兼** N1 concurrently, and 同时	**聖** N1 holy, saint, sage, master, priest 圣	**旨** N1 delicious, relish, show a liking for, purport, will 美味的
即 N1 instant, namely, as is, conform, agree, adapt 瞬间	**柳** N1 willow 柳	**舎** N1 cottage, inn, hut, house, mansion 山寨	**偽** N1 falsehood, lie, deceive, pretend, counterfeit 谬误
較 N1 contrast, compare 比较	**覇** N1 hegemony, supremacy, leadership, champion 霸权	**詳** N1 detailed, full, minute, accurate, well-informed 详细	**抵** N1 resist, reach, touch 抗
脅 N1 threaten, coerce 威胁	**茂** N1 overgrown, grow thick, be luxuriant 杂草丛生	**犠** N1 sacrifice 牺牲	**旗** N1 national flag, banner, standard 旗
距 N1 long-distance 距离	**雅** N1 gracious, elegant, graceful, refined 优雅	**飾** N1 decorate, ornament, adorn, embellish 装饰	**網** N1 netting, network 网络

N1	N1	N1	N1
竜	**詩**	**繁**	**翼**
dragon, imperial	poem, poetry	luxuriant, thick, overgrown, frequency, complexity	wing, plane, flank
龙	诗歌	复杂	翅膀

N1	N1	N1	N1
潟	**敵**	**魅**	**嫌**
lagoon	enemy, foe, opponent	fascination, charm, bewitch	dislike, detest, hate
泻湖	敌人	魅力	疑似

N1	N1	N1	N1
斉	**敷**	**擁**	**圏**
adjusted, alike, equal, similar variety of	spread, pave, sit, promulgate	hug, embrace, possess, protect, lead	sphere, circle, radius, range
已调整	传播	拥抱	球

N1	N1	N1	N1
酸	**罰**	**滅**	**礎**
acid, bitterness, sour, tart	penalty, punishment	destroy, ruin, overthrow, perish	cornerstone, foundation stone
酸	惩治	破坏	基础

N1	N1	N1	N1
腐	**潮**	**梅**	**尽**
rot, decay, sour	tide, salt water, opportunity	plum	exhaust, use up, run out of, befriend, serve
腐烂	浪潮	李子	排气

Kanji	Meaning	Chinese
僕 (N1)	me, I (male)	我
桜 (N1)	cherry	樱桃
滑 (N1)	slippery, slide, slip, flunk	滑
孤 (N1)	orphan, alone	孤儿
炎 (N1)	inflammation, flame, blaze	炎
賠 (N1)	compensation, indemnify	补偿金
句 (N1)	phrase, clause, sentence, passage, paragraph	短语
鋼 (N1)	steel	钢
頑 (N1)	stubborn, foolish, firmly	顽固
鎖 (N1)	chain, irons, connection	链
彩 (N1)	coloring, paint, makeup	染色
摩 (N1)	chafe, rub, polish, grind, scrape	抛光
励 (N1)	encourage, be diligent, inspire	鼓励
縦 (N1)	vertical, length, height, self-indulgent, wayward	垂直
輝 (N1)	radiance, shine, sparkle, gleam, twinkle	辉煌
蓄 (N1)	amass, keeping a concubine, phonograph	留声机
軸 (N1)	axis, pivot, stem, stalk, counter for book scrolls	轴
巡 (N1)	patrol, go around, circumference	巡逻
稼 (N1)	earnings, work, earn money	收益
瞬 (N1)	wink, blink, twinkle	眨眼

N1	N1	N1	N1
砲 cannon, gun 枪	噴 erupt, spout, emit, flush out 喷雾	誇 boast, be proud, pride, triumphantly 夸	祥 auspicious, happiness, good omen 吉祥
牲 animal sacrifice, offering 牺牲	秩 regularity, salary, order 薪水	帝 sovereign, the emperor, god, creator 皇帝	宏 wide, large 宽
唆 tempt, seduce, instigate, promote 诱惑	阻 thwart, separate from, prevent, obstruct, deter 避免	泰 peaceful, calm, peace, easy, Thailand 平静的	賄 bribe, board, supply, finance 贿赂
撲 slap, strike, hit, beat, tell, speak 耳光	堀 ditch, moat, canal 沟渠	菊 chrysanthemum 菊花	絞 strangle, constrict, wring 扼杀
縁 affinity, relation, connection, edge, border 亲和力	唯 solely, only, merely, simply 只要	膨 swell, get fat, thick 胀	矢 dart, arrow 镖

N1	N1	N1	N1
耐	**塾**	**漏**	**慶**
-proof, enduring	cram school, private school	leak, escape, time	jubilation, congratulate, rejoice, be happy
持久	私立学校	泄漏	庆祝
猛	**芳**	**懲**	**剣**
fierce, rave, rush, become furious, wildness	perfume, balmy, flavorable, fragrant	penal, chastise, punish, discipline	sabre, sword, blade, clock hand
激烈	香水	刑事	剑
彰	**棋**	**丁**	**恒**
patent, clear	chess piece, Japanese chess, shogi	street, ward, town	constancy, always
专利	棋	街	不变
揚	**冒**	**之**	**倫**
hoist, fry in deep fat	risk, face, defy, dare, damage, assume (a name)	of, this	ethics, companion
提升	风险	这个	伴侣
陳	**憶**	**梨**	**仁**
exhibit, state, relate, explain	recollection, think, remember	pear tree	humanity, virtue, benevolence, charity, man, kernel
展示	召回	梨	仁

N1	N1	N1	N1
克	**岳**	**概**	**拘**
overcome, kindly, skillfully	point, peak, mountain	outline, condition, approximation, generally	arrest, seize, concerned, adhere to, despite
克服	点	大纲	逮捕
墓	**黙**	**須**	**偏**
grave, tomb	silence, become silent, stop speaking, leave as is	ought, by all means, necessarily	partial, side, left-side radical, inclining, biased
墓	安静	一定	部分的
雾	**遇**	**諮**	**狭**
atmosphere, fog	interview, treat, entertain, receive, deal with	consult with	cramped, narrow, contract, tight
大气层	面试	请教	狭窄
卓	**亀**	**糧**	**簿**
eminent, table, desk, high	tortoise, turtle	provisions, food, bread	register, record book
杰出	龟	粮食	寄存器
炉	**牧**	**殊**	**殖**
hearth, furnace, kiln, reactor	breed, care for, shepherd, feed, pasture	particularly, especially, exceptionally	augment, increase, multiply, raise
炉	品种	特别	增加

艦 — warship — 军舰

輩 — comrade, fellow, people, companions — 同志

穴 — hole, aperture, slit, cave, den — 孔

奇 — strange, strangeness, curiosity — 奇

慢 — ridicule, laziness — 嘲笑

鶴 — crane, stork — 起重机

謀 — conspire, cheat, impose on, plan, devise, scheme — 合谋

暖 — warmth — 温暖

昌 — prosperous, bright, clear — 繁荣

拍 — clap, beat (music) — 拍

朗 — melodious, clear, bright, serene, cheerful — 悠扬的

寬 — tolerant, leniency, generosity, relax, feel at home — 宽容

覆 — capsize, cover, shade, mantle, be ruined — 覆盖

胞 — placenta, sac, sheath — 鞘

泣 — cry, weep, moan — 泣

隔 — isolate, alternate, distance, separate, gulf — 隔离

浄 — clean, purify, cleanse, exorcise, Manchu Dynasty — 清洁

没 — drown, sink, hide, fall into, disappear, die — 淹

暇 — spare time, rest, leisure, time, leave of absence — 休闲

肺 — lungs — 肺

N1	N1	N1	N1
貞 upright, chastity, constancy, righteousness 直立	**靖** peaceful 平静的	**鑑** specimen, take warning from, learn from 标本	**飼** domesticate, raise, keep, feed 驯化
陰 shade, yin, negative, sex organs, secret, shadow 阴影	**銘** inscription, signature (of artisan) 题词	**随** follow, though, notwithstanding 跟随	**烈** ardent, violent, vehement, furious, severe, extreme 热心
尋 inquire, fathom, look for 查询	**稿** draft, copy, manuscript, straw 草案	**丹** rust-colored, red, red lead, pills 红色	**啓** disclose, open, say 透露
也 to be (classical) 并且	**丘** hill, knoll 爬坡道	**壤** lot, earth, soil 泥	**漫** cartoon, involuntarily, in spite of oneself 动画片
玄 mysterious, occultness 神秘	**粘** sticky, glutinous, greasy, persevere 棒	**悟** enlightenment, perceive, discern, realize 启示	**舗** shop, store 店

妊 N1	熟 N1	旭 N1	恩 N1
pregnancy	mellow, ripen, mature, acquire skill	rising sun, morning sun	grace, kindness, goodness, favor, mercy
怀孕	醇美	太阳	善良
騰 N1	往 N1	豆 N1	遂 N1
inflation, advancing, going	journey, chase away, let go, going, travel	beans, pea, midget	consummate, accomplish, attain, commit (suicide)
通货膨胀	旅程	豆子	完善
狂 N1	岐 N1	陛 N1	緯 N1
lunatic, insane, crazy, confuse	branch off, fork in road, scene, arena, theater	highness, steps (of throne)	horizontal, woof, left & right, latitude
疯子	现场	高度	水平的
培 N1	衰 N1	艇 N1	屈 N1
cultivate, foster	decline, wane, weaken	rowboat, small boat	yield, bend, flinch, submit
培育	下降	船	弯曲
径 N1	淡 N1	抽 N1	披 N1
diameter, path, method	thin, faint, pale, fleeting	pluck, pull, extract, excel	expose, open
路径	苍白	采摘	暴露

廷 N1 courts, imperial court, government office 法院	**錦** N1 brocade, fine dress, honors 锦缎	**准** N1 quasi-, semi-, associate 关联	**暑** N1 sultry, hot, summer heat 热
磯 N1 seashore, beach 海滨	**奨** N1 exhort, urge, encourage 劝诫	**浸** N1 immersed, soak, dip, steep, moisten, wet, dunk 沉浸	**剰** N1 surplus, besides 剩余
胆 N1 gall bladder, courage, pluck, nerve 勇气	**繊** N1 slender, fine, thin kimono 苗条的	**駒** N1 pony, horse, colt 驹	**虚** N1 void, emptiness, unpreparedness, crack, fissure 空虚
霊 N1 spirits, soul 精神	**帳** N1 notebook, account book, album 笔记本	**悔** N1 repent, regret 后悔	**諭** N1 rebuke, admonish, charge, warn, persuade 训斥
惨 N1 wretched, disaster, cruelty, harsh 可怕	**虐** N1 tyrannize, oppress 压迫	**翻** N1 flip, turn over, wave, flutter, change (mind) 转	**墜** N1 crash, fall (down) 秋季

沼

marsh, lake, bog, swamp, pond

沼泽

据

set, lay a foundation, install, equip, squat down

根据

肥

fertilizer, get fat, fertile, manure, pamper

肥料

徐

gradually, slowly, deliberately, gently

逐渐

糖

sugar

糖

搭

board, load (a vehicle), ride

骑

盾

shield, escutcheon, pretext

屏蔽

脈

vein, pulse, hope

脉冲

滝

waterfall, rapids, cascade

瀑布

軌

rut, wheel, track, model, way of doing

发情

俵

bag, bale, sack, counter for bags

袋

妨

disturb, prevent, hamper, obstruct

干扰

擦

grate, rub, scratch, scrape, chafe, scour

擦

鯨

whale

鲸

荘

villa, inn, cottage, feudal manor

旅店

諾

consent, assent, agreement

同意

雷

thunder, lightening bolt

雷

漂

drift, float (on liquid)

漂移

懷

pocket, feelings, heart, yearn, miss someone

情怀

勘

intuition, perception

直觉

栽 N1	**拐** N1	**駄** N1	**添** N1
plantation, planting	kidnap, falsify	burdensome, pack horse, horse load, send by horse	annexed, accompany, marry, suit, meet
种植	绑架	繁重的	陪
冠 N1	**斜** N1	**鏡** N1	**聡** N1
crown, best, peerless	diagonal, slanting, oblique	mirror, speculum, barrel-head	wise, fast learner
王冠	对角线	镜子	明智的
浪 N1	**亜** N1	**覧** N1	**詐** N1
wandering, waves, billows	Asia, rank next, come after, -ous	perusal, see	lie, falsehood, deceive, pretend
波	亚洲	细读	谬误
壇 N1	**勲** N1	**魔** N1	**酬** N1
podium, stage, rostrum, terrace	meritorious deed, merit	witch, demon, evil spirit	repay, reward, retribution
讲台	值得	巫婆	偿还
紫 N1	**曙** N1	**紋** N1	**卸** N1
purple, violet	dawn, daybreak	family crest, figures	wholesale
紫色	黎明	图案	批发

N1	N1	N1	N1
奮	**欄**	**逸**	**涯**
stirred up, be invigorated, flourish	column, handrail, blank, space	deviate, idleness, leisure, miss the mark, evade	horizon, shore
繁荣	柱	偏离	地平线
拓	**眼**	**獄**	**尚**
clear (the land), open, break up (land)	eyeball	prison, jail	esteem, furthermore, still, yet
延期	眼睛	监狱	尊重
彫	**穏**	**顕**	**巧**
carve, engrave, chisel	calm, quiet, moderation	appear, existing	adroit, skilled, ingenuity
雕刻	平静	出现	独创性
矛	**垣**	**欺**	**萩**
halberd, arms, festival float	hedge, fence, wall	deceit, cheat, delude	bush clover
戟	树篱	欺骗	布什三叶草
粛	**栗**	**愚**	**遭**
solemn, quietly, softly	chestnut	foolish, folly, absurdity, stupid	encounter, meet, party, association, interview
庄严	板栗	笨	遭遇

架 N1	鬼 N1	庶 N1	稚 N1
erect, frame, mount, support, shelf, construct	ghost, devil	commoner, all, bastard	immature, young
帧	鬼	平民	幼稚
滋 N1	幻 N1	煮 N1	姫 N1
nourishing, more & more, be luxuriant	phantasm, vision, dream, illusion, apparition	boil, cook	princess
滋养	幻象	厨师	公主
誓 N1	把 N1	践 N1	呈 N1
vow, swear, pledge	grasp, faggot, bunch, counter for bundles	tread, step on, trample, practice, carry through	display, offer, present, send, exhibit
发誓	把握	实践	显示
疎 N1	仰 N1	剛 N1	疾 N1
alienate, rough, neglect, shun, sparse	face-up, look up, depend, seek, respect, rever	sturdy, strength	rapidly
离间	寻求	坚固	迅速地
征 N1	砕 N1	嫁 N1	謙 N1
subjugate, attack the rebellious, collect taxes	smash, break, crush, familiar, popular	marry into, bride	self-effacing, humble oneself, condescend
征服	粉碎	新娘	谦虚

后 N1 empress, queen, after, behind, back, later 皇后	**嘆** N1 sigh, lament, moan, grieve 叹	**菌** N1 germ, fungus, bacteria 菌	**鎌** N1 sickle, scythe, trick 镰刀
巢 N1 nest, rookery, hive, cobweb, den 巢	**頻** N1 repeatedly, recur 频率	**琴** N1 harp, koto 竖琴	**班** N1 squad, corps, unit, group 队
棚 N1 shelf, ledge, rack, mount, mantle, trellis 架	**潔** N1 undefiled, pure, clean, righteous, gallant 不de污	**酷** N1 cruel, severe, atrocious, unjust 残忍	**宰** N1 superintend, manager, rule 督
廊 N1 corridor, hall, tower 走廊	**寂** N1 loneliness, quietly, mellow, mature 孤独	**辰** N1 sign of the dragon, 7-9AM 龙	**霞** N1 be hazy, grow dim, blurred 模糊
伏 N1 prostrated, bend down, bow, cover, lay (pipes) 拜倒	**碁** N1 Go 走	**俗** N1 vulgar, customs, manners, worldliness 庸俗	**漠** N1 vague, obscure, desert, wide 沙漠

邪 N1	晶 N1	墨 N1	鎮 N1
wicked, injustice, wrong	sparkle, clear, crystal	black ink, India ink, ink stick, Mexico	tranquilize, ancient peace-preservation centers
邪恶	水晶	墨	镇定
洞 N1	履 N1	劣 N1	那 N1
den, cave, excavation	footgear, shoes, boots, put on (the feet	inferiority, be inferior to, be worse	what?
洞穴	鞋	下	什么?
殴 N1	娠 N1	奉 N1	憂 N1
assault, hit, beat, thrash	with child, pregnancy	observance, offer, present, dedicate	melancholy, grieve, lament, be anxious, sad
突击	孕	遵守	忧郁的
朴 N1	亭 N1	淳 N1	怪 N1
crude, simple, plain, docile	pavilion, restaurant, mansion, arbor, cottage	pure	suspicious, mystery, apparition
原油	亭	纯	可疑
鳩 N1	酔 N1	惜 N1	穫 N1
pigeon, dove	drunk, feel sick, poisoned, elated, spellbound	pity, be sparing of, frugal, stingy, regret	harvest, reap
鸽子	醉	可怜	收获

佳 N1 excellent, beautiful, good, pleasing, skilled 优秀	**潤** N1 wet, be watered, profit by, receive benefits 濡	**悼** N1 lament, grieve over 哀叹	**乏** N1 destitution, scarce, limited 贫穷
該 N1 above-stated, the said, that specific 具体	**赴** N1 proceed, get, become, tend 继续	**桑** N1 mulberry 桑	**桂** N1 Japanese Judas-tree, cinnamon tree 肉桂树
髄 N1 marrow, pith 骨髓	**虎** N1 tiger, drunkard 虎	**盆** N1 basin, lantern festival, tray 盆地	**晋** N1 advance 预先
穂 N1 ear, ear (grain), head, crest (wave) 耳	**壮** N1 robust, manhood, prosperity 强大	**堤** N1 dike, bank, embankment 堤围	**飢** N1 hungry, starve 饥饿
傍 N1 bystander, side, besides, while, nearby, 3rd person 旁观者	**疫** N1 epidemic 疫情	**累** N1 accumulate, involvement, trouble, tie up 积累	**痴** N1 stupid, foolish 白痴

搬 N1	晃 N1	癒 N1	寸 N1
conveyor, carry, transport	clear	healing, cure, quench (thirst), wreak	measurement, foot, 10
移动	明确	疗愈	测量
郭 N1	尿 N1	凶 N1	吐 N1
enclosure, quarters, fortification	urine	villain, evil, bad luck, disaster	spit, vomit, belch, confess, tell (lies)
外壳	尿	恶棍	吐
宴 N1	鷹 N1	賓 N1	虜 N1
banquet, feast, party	hawk	V.I.P., guest	captive, barbarian, low epithet for the enemy
宴会	鷹	客人	俘虏
陶 N1	鐘 N1	憾 N1	猪 N1
pottery, porcelain	bell, gong, chimes	remorse, regret, be sorry	boar
陶器	钟	后悔	猪
紘 N1	磁 N1	弥 N1	昆 N1
large	magnet, porcelain	all the more, increasingly	descendants, elder brother, insect
大	磁性	日益	子孙

N1	N1	N1	N1
粗	訂	芽	庄
coarse, rough, rugged	revise, correct, decide	bud, sprout, spear, germ	level
粗	修改	芽	水平
傘	敦	騎	寧
umbrella	industry, kindliness	equestrian, riding on horses	rather, preferably
雨伞	行业	马术	宁可
循	忍	怠	如
sequential, fellow	endure, bear, put up with, conceal, secrete	neglect, laziness	likeness, like, such as, as if, better, best, equal
顺序的	忍受	忽略	相似
寮	祐	鵬	鉛
dormitory, hostel, villa, tea pavillion	help	phoenix	lead
宿舍	救命	凤凰	铅
珠	苗	獸	哀
pearl, gem, jewel	seedling, sapling, shoot	animal, beast	pathetic, grief, sorrow, pathos, pity, sympathize
珍珠	幼苗	动物	可悲的

跳 N1 hop, leap up, spring, jerk, prance, buck, splash 跳	**匠** N1 artisan, workman, carpenter 工匠	**垂** N1 droop, suspend, hang, slouch 下垂	**蛇** N1 snake, serpent, hard drinker 蛇
澄 N1 lucidity, be clear, clear, clarify, settle, strain 明确	**縫** N1 sew, stitch, embroider 缝	**僧** N1 Buddhist priest, monk 僧	**眺** N1 stare, watch, look at, see, scrutinize 盯
亘 N1 span, request 跨度	**呉** N1 give, do something for 给	**凡** N1 mediocre 平庸	**憩** N1 recess, rest, relax, repose 凹进
媛 N1 beautiful woman, princess 公主	**溝** N1 gutter, ditch, sewer, drain, 10**32 天沟	**恭** N1 respect, reverent 尊重	**刈** N1 reap, cut, clip, trim, prune 收割
睡 N1 drowsy, sleep, die 昏昏欲睡	**錯** N1 confused, mix, be in disorder 困惑	**伯** N1 chief, count, earl, uncle, Brazil 首席	**笹** N1 bamboo grass 竹草

穀 — N1 cereals, grain 谷物	**陵** — N1 mausoleum, imperial tomb 陵	**霧** — N1 fog, mist 多雾路段	**魂** — N1 soul, spirit 灵魂
弊 — N1 abuse, evil, vice, breakage 滥用	**妃** — N1 queen, princess 女王	**舶** — N1 liner, ship 船	**餓** — N1 starve, hungry, thirst 饥饿
窮 — N1 hard up, destitute, suffer, perplexed, cornered 遭受	**掌** — N1 manipulate, rule, administer, conduct, palm of hand 操纵	**麗** — N1 lovely, companion 可爱	**綾** — N1 design, figured cloth, twill 设计
臭 — N1 stinking, ill-smelling, suspicious looking 臭	**悦** — N1 ecstasy, joy, rapture 很高兴	**刃** — N1 blade, sword, edge 刀	**縛** — N1 truss, arrest, bind, tie, restrain 桁架
曆 — N1 calendar, almanac 日历	**宜** — N1 best regards, good 最好的祝福	**盲** — N1 blind, blind man, ignoramus 盲	**粋** — N1 chic, style, purity, essence, pith, cream, elite 别致的

辱 N1 embarrass, humiliate, shame 尴尬的	**毅** N1 strong 强大	**轄** N1 control, wedge 控制	**猿** N1 monkey 猴
弦 N1 bowstring, chord, hypotenuse 弦	**稔** N1 harvest, ripen 收成	**窒** N1 plug up, obstruct 阻碍	**炊** N1 cook, boil 烹饪
洪 N1 deluge, flood, vast 洪水	**摂** N1 vicarious, surrogate, act in addition to 替代的	**飽** N1 sated, tired of, bored, satiate 累	**冗** N1 superfluous, uselessness 多余
桃 N1 peach tree 桃子	**狩** N1 hunt, raid, gather 狩猎	**朱** N1 vermilion, cinnabar, scarlet, red, bloody 朱红	**渦** N1 whirlpool, eddy, vortex 涡流
紳 N1 sire, good belt, gentleman 绅士	**枢** N1 hinge, pivot, door 合页	**碑** N1 tombstone, monument 纪念碑	**鍛** N1 forge, discipline, train 锻造

刀 N1 sword, saber, knife 剑	**鼓** N1 drum, beat, rouse, muster 鼓	**裸** N1 naked, nude, uncovered, partially clothed 裸	**猶** N1 furthermore, still, yet 此外
塊 N1 clod, lump, chink, clot, mass 凝块	**旋** N1 rotation, go around 回转	**弓** N1 bow, bow (archery, violin) 弓	**幣** N1 cash, bad habit, humble prefix, gift 现金
膜 N1 membrane 膜	**扇** N1 fan, folding fan 风扇	**腸** N1 intestines, guts, bowels, viscera 肠	**槽** N1 vat, tub, tank 增值税
慈 N1 mercy 怜悯	**楊** N1 willow 柳	**伐** N1 fell, strike, attack, punish 跌倒了	**駿** N1 a good horse, speed, a fast person 速度
糾 N1 twist, ask, investigate, verify 捻	**亮** N1 clear, help 亮	**墳** N1 tomb, mound 坟墓	**坪** N1 two-mat area, ~36 sq ft 平

紺 N1	娛 N1	舌 N1	羅 N1
dark blue, navy	recreation, pleasure	tongue, reed, clapper	gauze, thin silk, Rome
蓝色	娱乐	舌	纱布
峽 N1	俸 N1	厘 N1	峰 N1
gorge, ravine	stipend, salary	rin, 1, 10sen, 1, 10bu	summit, peak
峡谷	薪水	厘米	峰
圭 N1	釀 N1	蓮 N1	弔 N1
square jewel, corner, angle, edge	brew, cause	lotus	condolences, mourning, funeral
角	酿造	莲花	慰问
乙 N1	汁 N1	尼 N1	遍 N1
the latter, duplicate, strange, witty	soup, juice, broth, sap, gravy, pus	nun	everywhere, times, widely, generally
重复	果汁	尼姑	到处
衡 N1	薰 N1	獵 N1	羊 N1
equilibrium, measuring rod, scale	send forth fragrance, fragrant, be scented	game-hunting, shooting, game, bag	sheep
平衡	香	射击	羊

款 N1 goodwill, article, section, friendship, collusion 善意	**閲** N1 review, inspection, revision 评论	**偵** N1 spy 间谍	**喝** N1 hoarse, scold 嘶哑
敢 N1 daring, sad, tragic, pitiful, frail, feeble 敢	**胎** N1 womb, uterus 子宫	**酵** N1 fermentation 酵母	**豚** N1 pork, pig 猪肉
遮 N1 intercept, interrupt, obstruct 截距	**扉** N1 front door, title page, front page 前门	**硫** N1 sulphur 硫	**赦** N1 pardon, forgiveness 赦免
窃 N1 stealth, steal, secret, private, hushed 偷	**泡** N1 bubbles, foam, suds, froth 气泡	**瑞** N1 congratulations 恭喜	**又** N1 or again, furthermore, on the other hand 此外
慨 N1 rue, be sad, sigh, lament 慷慨	**紡** N1 spinning 纺纱	**恨** N1 regret, bear a grudge, resentment, malice, hatred 后悔	**肪** N1 obese, fat 肥胖的

扶 N1	戯 N1	伍 N1	忌 N1
aid, help, assist	frolic, play, sport	5, 5-man squad, file, line	mourning, abhor, detestable, death anniversary
救命	嬉戏	线	丧

濁 N1	奔 N1	斗 N1	蘭 N1
voiced, uncleanness, wrong, nigori, impurity	bustle, run	Big Dipper, 10 sho (vol), sake dipper	orchid, Holland
不洁	跑	桶	兰花

迅 N1	肖 N1	鉢 N1	朽 N1
swift, fast	resemblance	bowl, rice tub, pot, crown	decay, rot, remain in seclusion
快速	相似	碗	烂

殻 N1	享 N1	秦 N1	茅 N1
husk, nut shell	receive, undergo, answer (phone), take, get, catch	Manchu dynasty	miscanthus reed
稻壳	经历	满族	黄can芦苇

藩 N1	沙 N1	輔 N1	媒 N1
clan, enclosure	sand	help	mediator, go-between
外壳	砂	辅助的	调解员

<table>
<tr>
<td>

鶏 _{N1}

chicken

鸡

</td>
<td>

禅 _{N1}

Zen, silent meditation

冥想

</td>
<td>

嘱 _{N1}

entrust, request, send a message

委托

</td>
<td>

胴 _{N1}

trunk, torso, hull (ship), hub of wheel

躯干

</td>
</tr>
<tr>
<td>

迭 _{N1}

transfer, alternation

传递

</td>
<td>

挿 _{N1}

insert, put in, graft, wear (sword)

插入

</td>
<td>

嵐 _{N1}

storm, tempest

风暴

</td>
<td>

椎 _{N1}

oak, mallet

橡木

</td>
</tr>
<tr>
<td>

絹 _{N1}

silk

丝

</td>
<td>

陪 _{N1}

obeisance, follow, accompany, attend on

服从

</td>
<td>

剖 _{N1}

divide

划分

</td>
<td>

譜 _{N1}

musical score, music, note, staff, table, genealogy

音乐

</td>
</tr>
<tr>
<td>

郁 _{N1}

cultural progress, perfume

香水

</td>
<td>

悠 _{N1}

permanence, distant, long time, leisure

永久性

</td>
<td>

淑 _{N1}

graceful, gentle, pure

优美

</td>
<td>

帆 _{N1}

sail

帆

</td>
</tr>
<tr>
<td>

暁 _{N1}

daybreak, dawn, in the event

黎明

</td>
<td>

傑 _{N1}

greatness, excellence

伟大

</td>
<td>

楠 _{N1}

camphor tree

樟树

</td>
<td>

笛 _{N1}

flute, clarinet, pipe, whistle, bagpipe, piccolo

长笛

</td>
</tr>
</table>

玲 N1	奴 N1	錠 N1	拳 N1
sound of jewels	guy, slave, manservant, fellow	lock, fetters, shackles	fist
珠宝	奴隶	锁	拳头
遷 N1	拙 N1	侍 N1	尺 N1
transition, move, change	bungling, clumsy, unskillful	waiter, samurai, wait upon, serve	shaku, Japanese foot, measure, scale, rule
移动	笨拙	服务员	测量
峠 N1	篤 N1	肇 N1	渇 N1
mountain peak, mountain pass, climax	fervent, kind, cordial, serious, deliberate	beginning	thirst, dry up, parch
高潮	热切	开始	口渴
叔 N1	雌 N1	亨 N1	堪 N1
uncle, youth	feminine, female	undergo, answer (phone), take, get, catch	withstand, endure, support, resist
叔叔	女	经历	值得
叙 N1	酢 N1	吟 N1	逓 N1
confer, relate, narrate, describe	vinegar, sour, acid, tart	versify, singing, recital	relay, in turn, sending
授予	尖酸刻薄	证明	中继

嶺 N1	甚 N1	喬 N1	崇 N1
peak, summit	tremendously, very, great, exceedingly	high, boasting	adore, respect, revere, worship
首脑	非常	吹牛	崇拜
漆 N1	岬 N1	癖 N1	愉 N1
lacquer, varnish, seven	headland, cape, spit, promontory	mannerism, habit, vice, trait, fault, kink	pleasure, happy, rejoice
涂料	岬	举止	请享用
寅 N1	礁 N1	乃 N1	洲 N1
sign of the tiger, 3-5AM	reef, sunken rock	from, possessive particle, whereupon, accordingly	continent, sandbar, island, country
虎	礁	从	大陆
屯 N1	樺 N1	槙 N1	姻 N1
barracks, police station, camp	birch	twig, ornamental evergreen	matrimony, marry
军营	桦木	枝条	婚姻
巌 N1	擬 N1	塀 N1	唇 N1
rock, crag, boulder	mimic, aim (a gun) at, nominate, imitate	fence, wall, (kokuji)	lips
岩石	模仿	围栏	唇

睦 N1 intimate, friendly, harmonious 亲密	**閑** N1 leisure 休闲	**胡** N1 barbarian, foreign 野蛮人	**幽** N1 seclude, confine to a room 隔离
峻 N1 high, steep 高	**曹** N1 cadet, friend 学员	**詠** N1 recitation, poem, song, composing 背诵	**卑** N1 lowly, base, vile, vulgar 卑微
侮 N1 scorn, despise, make light of, contempt 轻蔑	**鋳** N1 casting, mint 铸件	**抹** N1 rub, paint, erase 擦拭	**尉** N1 military officer, jailer, old man, rank 队长
隷 N1 slave, servant, prisoner, criminal, follower 奴隶	**禍** N1 calamity, misfortune, evil, curse 灾害	**蝶** N1 butterfly 蝴蝶	**酪** N1 dairy products, whey, broth, fruit juice 乳清
茎 N1 stalk, stem 干	**帥** N1 commander, leading troops, governor 指挥官	**逝** N1 departed, die 去世	**汽** N1 vapor, steam 汽

琢 N1	匿 N1	襟 N1	蛍 N1
polish	hide, shelter, shield	collar, neck, lapel	lightning-bug, firefly
抛光	隐藏	领	萤火虫
蕉 N1	寡 N1	琉 N1	痢 N1
banana	widow, minority, few	lapis lazuli	diarrhea
香蕉	寡妇	青金石	腹泻
庸 N1	朋 N1	坑 N1	藍 N1
commonplace, ordinary, employment	companion, friend	pit, hole	indigo
平凡	友人	坑	蓝色
賊 N1	搾 N1	畔 N1	遼 N1
burglar, rebel, traitor, robber	squeeze	paddy ridge, levee	distant
贼	挤	大堤	遥远
唄 N1	孔 N1	橘 N1	漱 N1
songs with samisen	cavity, hole, slit, very, great, exceedingly	mandarin orange	gargle, rinse mouth
呗	孔	柑橘	冲洗

N1	N1	N1	N1
呂	拷	嬢	苑
spine, backbone	torture, beat	lass, girl, Miss, daughter	garden, farm, park
脊柱	折磨	女孩	花园
N1	N1	N1	N1
巽	杜	渓	翁
southeast	woods, grove	mountain stream, valley	venerable old man
东南	树木	谷	老人
N1	N1	N1	N1
廉	謹	瞳	湧
bargain, reason, charge, suspicion	discreet, reverently, humbly	pupil	boil, ferment, seethe, uproar, breed
讨价还价	慎重	瞳孔	煮
N1	N1	N1	N1
欣	窯	褒	醜
take pleasure in, rejoice	kiln, oven, furnace	praise, extol	ugly, unclean, shame, bad looking
麾	窑	赞美	丑陋
N1	N1	N1	N1
升	煩	巴	禎
measuring box, 1.8 liter	anxiety, trouble, worry, pain, ill, annoy	comma-design	happiness
测量盒	焦虑	逗号	幸福

N1	N1	N1	N1
劾 censure, criminal investigation 谴责	**堕** degenerate, descend to, lapse into 退化	**租** tariff, crop tax, borrowing 出租	**稜** angle, edge, corner, power, majesty 边缘
桟 scaffold, cleat, frame, jetty, bolt (door) 脚手架	**倭** Yamato, ancient Japan 日本	**婿** bridegroom, son-in-law 新郎	**斐** beautiful, patterned 美丽
罷 quit, stop, leave, withdraw, go 停	**矯** rectify, straighten, correct, reform, cure 正确	**某** so-and-so, one, a certain, that person 某些	**囚** captured, criminal, arrest, catch 囚犯
魁 charging ahead of others 充电中	**虹** rainbow 彩虹	**鴻** large bird, wild goose 鹅	**泌** ooze, flow, soak in, penetrate, secrete 隐秘
於 at, in, on, as for 在	**赳** strong and brave 勇敢	**漸** steadily, gradually advancing, finally, barely 逐渐	**蚊** mosquito 蚊子

N1	N1	N1	N1
葵	厄	藻	禄
hollyhock	unlucky, misfortune, bad luck, disaster	seaweed, duckweed	fief, allowance, pension, grant, happiness
蜀葵	倒霉的	海藻	津贴

N1	N1	N1	N1
孟	嫡	堯	嚇
chief, beginning	legitimate wife, direct descent (non-bastard)	high, far	menacing, dignity, majesty, threaten
开始	第一任妻子	高	尊严

N1	N1	N1	N1
凸	暢	韻	霜
convex, beetle brow, uneven	stretch	rhyme, elegance, tone	frost
凸面	伸展	韵	霜

N1	N1	N1	N1
硝	勅	芹	杏
nitrate, saltpeter	imperial order	parsley	apricot
硝酸盐	英制	香菜	杏

N1	N1	N1	N1
棺	儒	鳳	馨
coffin, casket	Confucian	male mythical bird	fragrant, balmy, favourable
棺材	儒	凤凰	香

慧 N1	愁 N1	楼 N1	彬 N1
wise	distress, grieve, lament, be anxious	watchtower, lookout, high building	refined, gentle
明智的	苦恼	岗楼	温和
匡 N1	眉 N1	欽 N1	薪 N1
correct, save, assist	eyebrow	respect, revere, long for	fuel, firewood, kindling
正确	眉	尊重	汽油
褐 N1	賜 N1	嵯 N1	綜 N1
brown, woollen kimono	grant, gift, boon, results	steep, craggy, rugged	rule
棕色	授予	陡	规则
繕 N1	栓 N1	翠 N1	鮎 N1
darning, repair, mend, trim, tidy up, adjust	plug, bolt, cork, bung, stopper	green	freshwater trout, smelt
织补	插头	绿色	鲶鱼
榛 N1	凹 N1	艶 N1	惣 N1
hazelnut, filbert	concave, hollow, sunken	glossy, luster, glaze, polish, charm, colorful	all
榛	凹	光滑	所有

N1	N1	N1	N1
蔦	錬	隼	渚
vine, ivy	tempering, refine, drill, train, polish	falcon	strand, beach, shore
藤蔓	回火	鹘	岸
N1	**N1**	**N1**	**N1**
衷	逐	斥	稀
inmost, heart, mind, inside	pursue, drive away, chase, accomplish, attain	reject, retreat, recede, withdraw, repel, repulse	rare, phenomenal, dilute (acid)
多数情况	追求	拒绝	稀
N1	**N1**	**N1**	**N1**
芙	皋	雛	惟
lotus, Mt Fuji	swamp, shore	chick, squab, duckling, doll	consider, reflect, think
莲花	沼泽	小鸡	考虑
N1	**N1**	**N1**	**N1**
佑	耀	黛	渥
help, assist	shine, sparkle, gleam, twinkle	blackened eyebrows	kindness
助攻	闪耀	眉毛	善良
N1	**N1**	**N1**	**N1**
憧	宵	妄	惇
yearn after, long for, aspire to, admire, adore	wee hours, evening, early night	delusion, unnecessarily, without authority	sincere, kind, considerate
佩服	晚间	幻想	真诚

N1	N1	N1	N1
脩	甫	酌	蚕
dried meat	for the first time, not until	bar-tending, serving sake, the host, draw (water)	silkworm
干肉	只是	杓	蚕
N1	N1	N1	N1
嬉	蒼	暉	頒
glad, pleased, rejoice	blue, pale	shine, light	distribute, disseminate, partition, understand
麾	苍白	闪耀	分发
N1	N1	N1	N1
只	肢	檀	凱
only, free, in addition	limb, arms & legs	cedar, sandlewood, spindle tree	victory song
只要	肢	雪松	胜利之歌
N1	N1	N1	N1
彗	嗣	叶	汐
comet	heir, succeed	grant, answer	eventide, tide, salt water, opportunity
彗星	继承人	回答	浪潮
N1	N1	N1	N1
絢	朔	伽	畝
kimono design	conjunction (astronomy), first day of month	nursing, attending, entertainer	furrow, 30 tsubo, ridge, rib
华丽	连词	护理	畦

N1	N1	N1	N1
抄	**爽**	**黎**	**惰**
extract, selection, summary, copy, spread thin	refreshing, bracing, resonant, sweet, clear	dark, black, many	lazy, laziness
复制	令人耳目一新	暗	懒
蛮	**冴**	**旺**	**萌**
barbarian	be clear, serene, cold, skilful	flourishing, successful, beautiful, vigorous	show symptoms of, sprout, bud, malt
野蛮人	安详	芊芊	发芽
偲	**壱**	**瑠**	**允**
recollect, remember	I, one	lapis lazuli	license, sincerity, permit
回忆	一	青金石	执照
蒔	**鯉**	**弧**	**遥**
sow (seeds)	carp	arc, arch, bow	far off, distant, long ago
种子	鲤鱼	弧	远程
瑛	**附**	**彪**	**但**
sparkle of jewelry, crystal	affixed, attach, refer to, append	spotted, mottled, patterned, small tiger	however, but
水晶	连接	斑	但

綺 N1 figured cloth, beautiful 美丽	**芋** N1 potato 土豆	**茜** N1 madder, red dye, Turkey red 马德	**凌** N1 endure, keep (rain)out, stave off, tide over 忍受
皓 N1 white, clear 白色	**洸** N1 sparkling water 苏打水	**毬** N1 burr, ball 毛刺	**婆** N1 old woman, grandma, wet nurse 奶奶
緋 N1 scarlet, cardinal 猩红	**鯛** N1 sea bream, red snapper 鲷鱼	**怜** N1 wise 明智的	**邑** N1 village, rural community 村
倣 N1 emulate, imitate 模拟	**碧** N1 blue, green 绿色	**啄** N1 peck, pick up 啄	**穣** N1 good crops, prosperity 庄稼
酉 N1 west, bird, sign of the bird 西方	**倹** N1 frugal, economy, thrifty 节俭	**柚** N1 citron 香橼	**繭** N1 cocoon 茧

N1	N1	N1	N1
亦	詢	采	紗
also, again	consult with	dice, form, appearance, take, coloring	gauze, gossamer
也	请教	骰子	纱布
賦	眸	玖	弐
levy, ode, prose, poem, tribute, installment	pupil of the eye	beautiful black jewel, nine	two, second
征收	眼睛	九	二
錘	諄	倖	痘
weight, plumb bob, sinker	tedious	happiness, luck	pox, smallpox
重量	乏味	幸好	天花
笙	侃	裟	洵
a reed instrument	strong, just, righteous, peace-loving	Buddhist surplice	alike, truth
芦苇	强大	重复的	真的
爾	耗	昴	銑
you, thou, second person	decrease	the Pleiades	pig iron
您	减少	昴	铣削

N1	N1	N1	N1
莞	伶	碩	宥
reed used to cover tatami	actor	large, great, eminent	soothe, calm, pacify
芦苇	演员	大	安抚
N1	N1	N1	N1
溔	晏	伎	朕
deep and broad	late, quiet, sets (sun)	deed, skill	majestic plural, imperial we
深	晚的	技能	一世
N1	N1	N1	N1
迪	綸	且	竣
edify, way, path	thread, silk cloth	moreover, also, furthermore	end, finish
路径	线	此外	完成
N1	N1	N1	N1
晨	吏	燦	麿
morning, early	officer, an official	brilliant	I, you, (kokuji)
早上	官方	辉煌	一世
N1	N1	N1	N1
頌	箇	楓	琳
eulogy	counters for things	maple	jewel, tinkling of jewelry
颂	柜台	枫	宝石

N1	N1	N1	N1
梧	哉	澪	晟
Chinese parasol tree, phoenix tree	how, what, alas, (question mark)	water route, shipping channel	clear
凤凰树	怎么样	渠道	明确

N1	N1	N1	N1
衿	凪	梢	丙
neck, collar, lapel	lull, calm, (kokuji)	treetops, twig	third class, 3rd, 3rd calendar sign
颈部	平静	枝条	第三

N1	N1	N1	N1
颯	茄	勺	恕
suddenly, smoothly	eggplant	ladle, one tenth of a go, dip	excuse, tolerate, forgive
顺利	茄子	杓	借口

N1	N1	N1	N1
瑚	遵	瞭	燎
ancestral offering receptacle	abide by, follow, obey, learn	clear	burn, bonfire
珊瑚	跟随	明确	烧伤

N1	N1	N1	N1
虞	柊	侑	謁
uneasiness, fear, anxiety, concern	holly	urge to eat	audience, audience (with king)
恐惧	冬青	吃	听众

N1	N1	N1	N1
斤 axe, 1.32 lb, catty, counter for loaves of bread 斧头	嵩 be aggravated, grow worse, grow bulky, swell 胀	捺 press, print, affix a seal, stamp 按下	蓉 lotus 莲花
茉 jasmine 茉莉花	燿 shine 闪耀	誼 friendship, intimacy 友谊	冶 melting, smelting 冶炼
栞 bookmark, guidebook 书签	墾 ground-breaking, open up farmland 培育	勁 strong 强度	菖 iris 虹膜
椋 type of deciduous tree, grey starling 八哥	叡 intelligence, imperial 情报	胤 descendent, issue, offspring 后代	凜 cold, strict, severe 冷
亥 sign of the hog, 9-11PM 猪	爵 baron, peerage, court rank 男爵	脹 dilate, distend, bulge, fill out, swell 扩张	麟 Chinese unicorn, genius, giraffe, bright, shining 天才

莉 N1 jasmine 茉莉花	**汰** N1 luxury, select 豪华	**瑶** N1 beautiful as a jewel 宝石	**瑳** N1 polish 抛光
耶 N1 question mark 问号	**椰** N1 coconut tree 椰子	**絃** N1 string, cord, samisen music 串	**丞** N1 help 救命
璃 N1 glassy, lapis lazuli 玻璃	**奎** N1 star, god of literature 星	**塑** N1 model, molding 模子	**昂** N1 rise 上升
柾 N1 straight grain, spindle tree, (kokuji) 粮食	**熙** N1 bright, sunny, prosperous, merry 亮	**菫** N1 the violet 紫色	**諒** N1 fact, reality, understand, appreciate 了解
鞠 N1 ball 球	**崚** N1 towering in a row 参天	**濫** N1 excessive, overflow, spread out 过多	**捷** N1 victory, fast 快

www.ingramcontent.com/pod-product-compliance
Lightning Source LLC
Chambersburg PA
CBHW080008180726
48002CB00021B/3164